# Second Annual
# Northwoods Anthology

### Robert W. Olmsted, editor

Cover by Lori Lane

Northwoods Press

The Poets' Press
Thomaston, Maine
U.S.A.

# Contents

*William Locke Hauser*
*Fort Lauderdale, FL*

# The Sisters

I thought of them as sisters, though one was perhaps the mother, being distinctly older than the other two, with deeper wrinkles scoring her cheeks. All possessed the same beaklike noses and sharp chins, shaping their profiles into crescent moons, and similar heads of frizzy dyed-red hair. Their clothing consisted of identical black dresses with girlishly short skirts in a synthetic material, topped with pastel-shaded cardigan wool sweaters, even in the heat of summer. Black shoes with thick heels and opaque flesh-colored stockings completed the ensemble.

They had their hair cut monthly in the same shop that I used, and insisted on the same barber named Carmine, who had emigrated from the very tip of Calabria. "You can see Sicily from my father's house," he would tell me, "and my great-grandfather, he was one of our renowned leader's officers." At this, he would nod reverently to a bust of Garibaldi on the counter arrayed with tonics and lotions. The jutting bearded chin and glaring eyes forbade any hint of disrespect.

One day the sisters had just preceded me into the shop, so I knew there was a long wait ahead. "Hold my place," I told Carmine, and went up the block for a *New York Times* and a latté from Starbucks. Returning, I settled down to read and sip.

The eldest was in the barber chair, while the others kibitzed from seats several away from where I waited. "A little more off the bottom," one called.

"But I favor it longer."

"For yourself maybe, but you tell me to keep mine short!" the third protested.

"Your head is shaped different. Your skull got squashed when you was a baby."

"I never . . ."

"What would you know about it?"

"I was there, wasn't I?"

"Not so's you'd remember."

On went the stream of chatter, contentious without being hostile, utterly devoid of humor. Too fascinated to concentrate on my paper, I used it as a screen to watch the show.

You see, I'm what you might call a "writer-voyeur," that is, I pick up most of my material from observing the world around me. Onhaitet's a town full of fascinating characters, like the man who weekly advertises in the local *Penny-Saver* for "persons with historical knowledge," to support his lifelong quest for justice. His French Catholic forebears, he says, were cheated out of extensive lands (now worth a king's ransom in this affluent New Jersey suburb) when the Protestant

British won the French and Indian War in 1763. "Spoils of war," various courts have ruled, but he continues to seek documentary evidence to the contrary. His only source thus far is the 1790 state charter, lost in an archives fire in 1912, which was quoted in periodicals of its time as restoring citizens' rights to "whatsoever Lands and Chattels of which they may have been deprived by the recently displaced and hateful Monarchy."

And there's the former business executive, let go by a top-named international corporation ("departed to pursue other interests," in the usual company-speak), who appears at Kevin's Diner every morning at precisely 6:30, orders the same breakfast from waitress Wanda (two-decades-back the "Prom Queen of Onhaitet High," with a trophy behind the cash register to prove it), and departs at exactly 6:55 to catch the 7:03 train. He walks to the station platform, mingles with a crowd of similarly dark-suited commuters, boards one end of a car and gets off the other, and drives to his yacht club to spend the day in its reading room. His wife, an alcoholic recluse, has no idea he's not still employed.

I could relate a dozen more, equally interesting. All grist for the mill.

I began to track those sisters (the *Weird Sisters* I conjectured, but dismissed the term as plagiaristic) on their rounds — breakfast at Kevin's, semi-weekly grocery shopping at Safeway, drop-ins at Sunshine Novelties & Sundries, the monthly haircuts with Carmine— intermittently, so as not to be obvious. It was so easy, for they held to a predictable schedule. Whether they suspected my purpose, I couldn't tell, but they eventually recognized that they and I were frequenters of the same merchants and, thereby, associates of a sort.

"Good day, young man," the oldest would say whenever they passed. The others would repeat, "Good day, young man." I would affect a little bow. "Good day, ladies."

And so it went for the better part of a year. They lived about halfway down the hill from rail station to lakeside park, in the second story of a Victorian house that had seen better days, the first floor being rented by an immigrant-labor family of indeterminate numbers. The shrubbery appeared to be trimmed professionally, but what had formerly been flowerbeds were now scuffed rectangles of dirt edged with rusted scallops of wire once painted white. The lawn was dotted with sickly tufts of grass, infrequently mowed.

If they worked, I could see no sign of it, other than occasional selling of handmade pottery from their home kiln at local street fairs. None of them drove, nor ever to my knowledge rode any public conveyance. Emerging around mid-morning, they conducted their joint errands, then disappeared back into the house about lunchtime. They looked well fed, stocky despite the narrowness of their faces, and healthy. I grew bored. Just a widow and her two maiden-lady daughters, living off a meager trust fund. No story there.

What sort of writing do I do? I'm a freelancer. You know the features you find in airline magazines — "Savannah at Christmas," "Nine Steps To A Happy Father-Son Relationship," "Trim Those Hips Through Bicycling"? I write a few like those, along with the typical "Get Killer Abs Fast!" for the muscle mags, and an occasional "Eternal-Life Pill Suppressed By Government!" for the checkout-counter tabloids. I'll never get rich, but it's steady work, with lots of variety. And this is such a nice town to live in, with an inexhaustible supply of material. I also do an occasional short story like this one, usually fiction (most of my non-fiction is fiction, if you want the absolute truth), but this story is real so help me God.

One October morning I was eating later than customary at Kevin's, when in walked the sisters. They chattered their way to the usual booth, behind me so I couldn't see them, but as I said I'd quit caring. Wanda came to take my order. "You've got friends," she said. "They want you to join them for breakfast."

"You're kidding. They never socialize with anyone."

"Better go," she smirked. "If you don't, they'll start caterwauling, and Kevin hates noise." I looked toward the kitchen, where the proprietor stood over his grill. Pointing to me, he jerked his head toward where the three were sitting. He was grinning, but I couldn't see the joke. "Oh what the hell," I muttered and got up, carrying my coffee with me.

"Good day, young man," the eldest said. "Good day, young man," echoed the pair.

What followed may be the strangest conversation I've ever had in my life. First off, they wanted to know everything about me — if my parents were living or had gone to "join the saints," whether I'd had a "normal" childhood, what my interests were (I omitted to mention writing), did I "like young ladies"? Each of my answers was greeted with a magisterial nod from the old one and suppressed giggles from the other two. They reciprocated by sharing their views on American society and the state of the world, the evils of meat consumption and which vegetarian foods were most healthy, and their determination, even as children, never to let a dog lick their faces.

Apparently satisfied by my non-disagreement with their many prejudices and complexes, the oldest leaned back against the booth cushions and pronounced a momentous decision: "You must come to tea."

I couldn't very well say no. "Wh-when?" I sputtered.

"At teatime, of course. Four o'clock this afternoon."

Feeling like Don Giovanni invited to dinner with the *Commandetore*, I feigned a delighted acceptance.

At the precise hour, before I could raise the heavy bronze lizard-shaped knocker, the door opened with a rasping screech like on some old recording of "The Inner Sanctum." And —I'm not making this up— there was no one there, only a dark stairway leading to the second floor.

Climbing up, I found myself in a rather conventional, if old-fashioned, living room. The floor was covered with once fine but now threadbare oriental rugs, there was a cherrywood chest that my mother would have killed for, several small tables in lustrous dark wood, and two loveseats with curlicued wood edging, covered in lavender velvet rubbed smooth in the places where a person's back would rest. The room was lighted by a pair of Tiffany lamps that, if originals, must have been worth a fortune. The air was thick with that "old house" smell.

There was a fireplace, a black hole empty of ornamentation, framed within an ornately carved mantel. On its top stood a pair of helical brass candlesticks and a row of Chinese export-porcelain covered jars.

After waving me to one of the loveseats while she took the other, the older woman engaged me in uneventful talk as the two younger fetched tea things. Earl Grey, choice of milk and lemon, brown and white sugar cubes, cucumber and liver-pâté sandwiches with the crusts removed —I was transported back to my grandmother's on a Sunday after church.

She noticed I was eyeing the jars. "Are you acquainted with porcelain, young man?"

"Yes, ma'am. An aunt of mine was a collector of Chinese export. These of yours are really very good."

"They are precious," she answered, "ain't they, girls?"

"They are precious indeed!" they chortled. "The one on right is Father."

"And the next holds brother Frederick," the old one said. "And the next is our little Sammy. We miss him, don't we, girls?" Heads nodded in unison.

"And the next," she said portentously, "is that awful man what made Grace sad by not marrying her."

"And the last?" I couldn't resist asking.

"Is the bastard what made her sad by marrying her."

The taller (by perhaps an inch) of the two younger women sniffled and put a handkerchief to her eyes. The shorter (I never did learn her name) curved an arm around her sister's shoulders and squeezed affectionately.

Suddenly feeling woozy, I tried to stand. My vision blurred, my legs turned to jelly, and I sat heavily back down.

I woke to find myself in a windowless, bare room, with no light other than what came through an open door. My hands were tied behind the back of a straight chair and I was unable to move my feet. The oldest, seated an arm's length away, was grimacing. "This is our music room," she said, "soundproofed by father so's the neighbors wouldn't be bothered by us girls' practicing. There's no point in you crying out. You can't even stomp your feet, because we've nailed your shoes to the floor."

"What are you going to do with me?"

"Starve you to death, then reduce the leavings in our pottery kiln. No violence. We don't hold with violence."

"But I've done nothing to you."

"Pried and spied. That's enough."

"Is this what happened to . . ."

"Yes." She walked out, closing the door behind her, leaving me in utter darkness.

I don't know how long I remained there, only that I wet and messed my pants, felt hunger and then excruciating thirst, and began to have hallucinations —dragons, witches, people I hadn't seen or thought of in years. They chanted a litany of my sins— the time I'd snitched a candy bar from the refreshment stand at the movie theater and let another boy take the rap, the book report on *Mansfield Park* I'd plagiarized for an A in English Lit, the girl I'd got pregnant and bullied into an abortion and then dumped, the five hundred I'd borrowed from my brother and conveniently forgotten to pay back. In one of those spells I imagined the door opening and someone forcing a cool liquid down my throat, spilling wetness onto my shirtfront.

It was breaking dawn when I next awoke, barefoot grimy and bristle-chinned, on my back amidst a grove of trees in the park. There was a breeze, and I could hear the dry rustling of autumn leaves and the slurp-slurp of ripples on the shore of the lake. From a distance came a muttering of waterfowl and the eerie coo-coo-coo of a dove. I struggled to my feet, disgusted at my smell and the now-dried slime in my pants. Seeing no one about, I waded into the frigid water, stripped and washed all over, then put the wet clothes back on with a feeling of immense relief. I passed no one I knew on my way home. Before tumbling into bed, I glanced at my calendar watch. The time was half past six, and the date was five days since my ordeal with the sisters. I slept until late afternoon, woke and had a bite to eat, then slept again till morning.

It's a small town, and I can't help but run into them occasionally. Each time they never fail to chorus, "Good day, young man." I look down at the pavement and hurry on by.

*Franklin W. Marshall*
*Simsbury, CT*

## Lawn Care

In georgic mode we dress the vernal ground
And cultivate such plants as would create
A replica of our forebears' savannah:
A monoculture of apartments built
With lawns alive through animality
At variance with equatorial
Adaptions to a continent aglow
With light, intense, and grassland settlement,
Like cats that mimic strides of the giraffe,
Like vertical vernaculars of birds
That scan north versions of a tropic lake,
Where gene encoded through millennia
A drive persists to duplicate and farm
Geographies of early humankind,
Like herbal tracts whence flow botanicals,
Like garden rectangles that blush with green
Broadleaves like fans and filaments of chive,
Now prey to urban sprawl and market mews,
And towards integrity of mountain tops,
A mining muster would decapitate,
Toward salmon runs and esker home for beetles,
Toward keep and safeguard of coniferous
Plantations and rain forest realty
Around a caesar in his oval palace
Snarl councils of disputants rife with malice.

*Peter A. Olsson*
*Keene N.H.*

# Elephant Lady

My name is Ellen. I love elephants. I am fifty years old, but I look sixty-five. My legs are the size of elephant legs. The only fat, wrinkled, thick-legged old lady that anyone ever loved was Eleanor Roosevelt. They over-looked her body, and loved her mind and spirit. I have a mediocre mind and no spirit left. In fact, my mind feels like Chubby Checker doing the "Twist" in a swimming pool filled with molasses. My sense of humor disappeared six months ago, and my attitude makes accounts of menopause sound like Madonna's sex life. Speaking of sex life, that old wino downstairs doesn't even stop by with his elegant bottle of Thunderbird on Friday nights anymore. I can't get a good night's sleep with or without alcohol. I read an article in OPRAH`s magazine, and it said that depressed people lose their appetite. Actually, I cannot stop eating, even after my feet disappeared out of sight beyond the belly fat that forms a wide, quivering, natural apron around my former waistline.

My daughter Lucy loves me, but she doesn't know me. She seldom can stand me for more than twenty minutes. In America, few young people find an old person interesting. Lin Chang my now dead and former neighbor said that old people are respected in China. My daughter never even introduced herself to Lin Chang. Lucy loves me but she doesn't listen to me. I want to move to China. Lucy is a dumb bitch!

You say, 'How can I say that about my own daughter?' My first clue was, when it dawned on me that she didn't have the vaguest idea about how important my elephants are to me. Elephants are beautiful, powerful, intelligent and grace-ful. They are not clumsy and awkward. I love my elephants. They surround me and protect me. I have over one hundred elephants, and I love every one of them. They never forget me.

Anyway, my daughter did convince me to get free medical care at the VA Hospital for my headaches. Those five years in the navy when I got out of high school might be good for something. In the VA hospital system hey call it "Service Connection". I got so many headaches when I was in the navy. The navy doctors never could figure out what caused my headaches. I got a medical discharge from the navy with 10% "Service Connection". In other words, the US Navy caused 10% of my headaches in life.

Every time my daughter comes to visit me, I get a terrible headache. Every time I get a job and the boss makes unreasonable demands on me, I get a terrible headache. Thunderbird wine gives me a headache, but my elephants take my headache away within an hour. They comfort me in every room of my apartment.

The VA general doctors couldn't find out a physical cause for my headaches and wanted me to see a psychiatrist. It was free, so I went to the appointment. Dr. Nelson wasn't like those psychiatrists you see in movies or on TV. He didn't have a beard. He is young, good looking and he listened to me for almost a whole hour! I mean, he really listened! Have you ever had anyone listen to you with complete attention for a whole hour? It felt eerie. I liked his blue eyes and they looked straight at me. He listened to the names of all my elephants and didn't joke about whether I was a republican or not. I showed him my smallest elephant and a picture of my largest one. I could tell that he cared about me, but I really cannot tell you exactly why.

Dr. Nelson asked just a few questions and they were mainly about Lucy and me. Nelson thought I could get help with my headaches at the VA Day Hospital program. He said it would be tough for me at first, but he thought I had the guts to stick with it until I got better. He said that the day hospital uses individual therapy, group therapy and psychodrama to help people put their problems into words. Then people could figure out their own answers. The more I was able to put my feelings, anger and fears into words, said Nelson,—the less I would have to keep tension stored up in my neck and scalp muscles. I agreed to try the day hospital for three months. What the Hell, it was free.

The VA Hospital is huge, but off near the back gate is a small building with its own little parking lot. When I drove up I at least was able to park. I was early enough so that the white-lined parking spaces were not so filled up that I had to enter one space between two already parked cars. Phew!!

The Day Hospital receptionist was kind, supportive and helpful with all the paper work. Computers are supposed to decrease paper work, but they actually just generate it faster. In the Day Hospital there are groups A, B and C. I was put in therapy group B and it was a "Lulu". There were 19 members, twenty including me. Five were bald or balding WWII or Korean War Vets and six were longhaired Vietnam Vets, some of whom were still fighting "Post-War Rejection Syndrome." I told the young "Nam-Whiners", as I called them, that they should try being a woman abandoned after one year of marriage with a one-year-old baby by a big brave marine! I didn't say my piece until the very end of group so there were a few shocked stares. I got a couple of warm smiles but I never even got to trust anyone enough to mention my elephants. I did talk a little bit about Lucy during the next two group meetings.

## PSYCHODRAMA DAY AND ME

Thursdays were psychodrama day at the day hospital. Groups A, B, and C were all at the psychodrama together. That made thirty-six patients and about ten staff and students in the audience. The psychodrama director was a tall, over-weight psychiatrist with a warm smile and a relaxed style. His name was Simon Solomon. He sat in a chair up on a slightly elevated stage. He chatted with some of the patients he had worked with at previous psychodramas. Some of the guys talked about progress they were making as a result of work at previous psycho-dramas. Other patients spoke about on-going unresolved problems. Solomon urged them to work further on them in psychodrama or in their small group therapy sessions. I began to get a headache.

Solomon asked the group,

"Does anyone have a situation to work on today at psychodrama?"

There was a silence and Solomon must have noticed my frown and self-mes-saging of my forehead. Solomon looked at me sympathetically and asked, "Are you OK? You look worried. By the way, what's your name?"

I said,

"My name is Ellen. I have a headache, but don't want psychodrama."

I hoped my frown would send him in search of another victim.

Solomon softly said,

"Ellen, we find that headaches, stomachaches, backaches and other body symptoms can be worked with in psychodrama. Chuck, remember how we helped you with your pain in the neck?"

Chuck was a member of my group B. He was one that had a warm smile.

Chuck said, "Yeah Doc, and I still work for that hardass, but it is a little easier!"

Solomon turned to me and said,

"Ellen, come up here and sit by me and we will talk a little about your head-aches."

Dr. Nelson had told me about this stuff. I found myself shuffling up to the stage with some curiosity and a lot of fear. Solomon quickly discovered with me that my last headache had been yesterday. As usual, it was during a visit with Lucy. Solomon said that it was important to set -the- scene in great detail, in my house where Lucy and I had argued.

I remember picturing my living room and saying,

"Now let me see——here is the table, there is the sofa, my TV, a small bookshelf and three of my elephants. Lucy was in the comfortable chair as usual and...."

Solomon interrupted me and said,

"Tell me more about your elephants?"

He looked curious.

I said,

"That's not important."

Solomon said that my face had softened and my neck was more relaxed looking when I mentioned the elephants, (MY Elephants).

I stopped paying attention to the other patients like they were a hundred yards away. I explained to Solomon that I had 157 elephants. They were all over my house. They are made of stone, wood, metal, silver, gold, cut glass, crystal, plastic and ivory. The one in the corner of my living room was four feet tall and had been carved by my father. He gave it to me for my nineteenth birthday and to celebrate my joining the Navy. My dad had been in the Navy and never forgot to bring me an elephant when he came back from a tour of duty. If he was gone on my birthday, he never forgot to mail me one——Special. I explained to Solomon that my dad died after my second year in the Navy and right before Lucy was born.

Now it started to get weird and scary. Solomon set up chairs and tables like it was my house. He asked a nurse to play the role of Lucy. He asked one of the "Nam Whiners" in my group to play my TV set. Solomon got my group buddy Chuck to play the 4-foot wooden elephant in the corner.

The scene started with the TV news going:

"Today the president meets with his economic advisors about Medicare benefits. Later today, he will fly on *Airforce One* to...."

The doorbell rang and it was Lucy.

"...The west coast was hit by heavy rains...mud slides..."

Lucy said with annoyance,

"Mom you can shut that damn TV off, it's on so loud, and all the time here."

(It actually felt good when Solomon let me go over and actually turn it off and shut up the "Nam Whiner" turned TV set actor).

I said, "I get lonely and you don't visit me much. The TV and my elephants are my only company. And, when you fuss at me I get a headache after you are here."

Lucy erupted,

"Mom, your damn elephants are weird. It is embarrassing for me to even bring a friend with me. They are all over this small house. That big one over there is ugly and the oil you put on it smells!"

(My head was really hurting now).

Chuck who was playing the large wood elephant and with prompting whispers from Solomon, spoke up forcefully,

"Ellen, tell Lucy who I am, NOW!"

I burst into tears, then sobs.

Solomon froze the scene briefly and had two nursing students gently massage my tense neck and forehead as Solomon explained,

"Ellen, Lucy might or might not know the source of your elephants, but it seems clear that she doesn't know their deep and important meaning to you. Lets have you try to talk to Lucy about this."

Solomon had me return to this scene repeatedly in efforts to help me talk to Lucy. Solomon had me reverse roles with Lucy, the wood elephant and then back to myself again. I cried, I giggled and I yelled at Lucy. I even pounded on a pillow named Lucy. (A key prop at many psychodramas, I would later learn).

The most moving part was when Chuck spoke in-role as the big wood elephant. He spoke gently but firmly directly to Lucy,

"Lucy, in a real way I am your grandfather. My name is Carl and I love(d) your mother very much. You are your mom's only daughter, just like she was mine. You never knew me, because I died when you were very little."

I interrupted Chuck's soliloquy, (Big psychodrama word I learned),

"Lucy, I never wanted to burden you with all the grief about your grandpa. You know I tried not to put all the hate of your dad on to you!"

The nurse in-role as Lucy said, "But Mom, I never knew these things. In fact it seems like we never talk about anything important."

Now I was really boo-hooing hard. The group and Solomon were real respectful. They let me cry for quite awhile. I told the group that my dad had been wise and never forgot me

"Like an elephant", someone gently said.

I went on to say that my dad had been too heavy, and his overweight caused his early heart-death. I am too heavy and feel blundering, lumbering and have big sad ears and eyes. Only, I hear and see sad things.

Solomon suggested that we return to the scene to see what Lucy thought now. I took Lucy's role and the nurse playing my role asked, "So what would you like for us to talk about?"

I in Lucy's role suddenly said, "Roller skate. When I was little we used to go all the time. You could lose weight that way Mom."

    Then that crazy, gentle, silly, bastard Solomon had us move all the chairs near the walls. We all started to pretend to roller skate around and around the group room. A giggling "Nam Whiner" played his harmonica to sound like organ music. Everyone was chuckling, crying and I never have felt so close to a bunch of people since I was a little girl in church. I felt emotionally exhausted but my headache was gone!

    Several mother/daughter family sessions helped the real Lucy and I to struggle to connect. After many months and a bunch of roller skating time, I am a smaller but wiser elephant.

*   *   *

### Patricia Craddock
### Lawrenceville, GA

## Earth Watch

Amid wars and rumors of war, our pastime of self against self,
we try to understand the meaning of it all. from Afghanistan
to Zaire, Bosnia, Ireland, Israel, Iraq, Palestine....
Nature, too, is beyond our control.
Floods cover half the earth, drought over the rest.
Earthquakes, tornadoes, hurricanes, storms....
All the shocks we are heir to, man-made and Divine.
Stunned, we can but wondering turn
away from the far to the near
away from the great to the small
away from the many back to one's own
struggle, like Jacob, with God.

* * *

Dripping water and sweat from this pitiless southern sun
I carry drinking pans to a parched field nearby
to succor the birds and the wild things watching,
beaks, mouths agape too hot to flee, to fly.
My reward? Watching a family of crows with their young
stepping in and out, dipping to drink and bathe.
Seeing my all too human need to play God,
somehow to confer life above death
upon those over whom I am given dominion.

Sometimes, for all our compassion we are overcome
with trying to save the whole world.
We discover that we are not God, after all,
and we do the little we can.

*Sheryl L. Nelms*
*Azle, TX*

## Saint Croix, Virgin Islands: Talk to Me Man

I sit on the hotel balcony
absorb the twitter
of canaries

as mango juice drips
from my chin

I spoon into the ripe papaya
drizzled with squeezed
lime

nibble a kiwi slice

pulled from a ring
of sweet pineapple

sip strawberry daiquiris
one by one

through the fan
churned afternoon heat

smell the lusciousness of passion flower blooming below

feel the thick clunk
of coconuts
being

harvested

and I become
turquoise

## Norman H Russell
### Edmond OK

### the indians

there are aliens among us
they have long hair red skin
piercing black eyes strong hands
they speak with the animals
and the white tops of mountains
in the forest they become trees
on the prairie they are grass
they are as old as the stones
and as young as the wind

they have always been with us
and were here long before us
and when we have gone our way
on our voyage into black space
they will remain behind
they will be here forever.

## Melanie Florence
### Fairfax, VA

### Cioppino

My mother lounges the afternoons away
on the powder blue couch in the sunniest room in the house,
engrossed in Sartre, or *The History of the World* or Monet.
Her short, curly black hair,
sometimes gray at the roots,
rests on propped pillows,
and her long legs stretch out on the couch,
with her foot tapping the air,
as she fills the time before dinner.

She rouses herself
in late afternoon,
and with shoeless feet,
she pads from the soft blue carpet
onto the cold brown kitchen tiles.

Not bothering to cover her flowing skirt with an apron
or take off her chunky jewelry,

she dives into cooking.
Now a whirlpool of motion,
out of the refrigerator
she pulls sea bass and halibut fillets,
shelled shrimp and lobster tails,
purchased fresh that morning from a local fish market.
Cans of tomatoes and spices soon encircle the stove
as she sautes onions and boils fish to make broth.
Last night she made New Mexico style chicken enchiladas,
tonight is Cioppino,
who knows what the dinner tomorrow would be?
She probably doesn't even know herself.

Humming tunelessly,
she sips white wine and stirs the soup,
while the kitchen counters overflow
with used dishes, spilled flour and drips of fish broth,
and the air wells up with the tangy aroma
of seafood, tomatoes and Italian spices.

After five, the rest of the household filters in,
returning home from their separate foragings.
First, my father in dress shirt and tie
steps in through the front door,
drapes his jacket on the stair banister,
and strides down the hallway that leads into the kitchen.

My mother tilts her head up to allow a peck on the cheek
and he pours himself a glass of wine
before heading to the television set in the next room,
where he waits, watching news or sports,
until my mother calls, "Dinner is ready."

The front door opens again
and two-year-old Brittni's quick footsteps
patter directly to my mother.
"Gramma, hold me," she cries, reaching up both arms.
My mother scoops her up, deposits her on a hip,
and sprinkles garlic on the buttered bread
as my brother paces back and forth,
across the kitchen tiles,
spouting out the litany of his day.

With her left hand closely securing her granddaughter,
my mother sets the table,
puts the garlic bread in the oven,

and sips her wine,
all with her right hand,
while she listens to my brother
and waits for the bread to toast.

## Joyce Mettelman
## Naples, FL

### ,Anniversaire

It isn't that two converge and become one:
It's that two stand close and remain two.
It isn't that our eyes focus on the same view:
It's that our two minds receive different messages
And translate for each other.
You help me to explore your worlds;
I show you paths you'd never chance alone.
Hand in hand or separately
We track the leaf-strewn forest;
Stand poised on the edge of a vast white snow bowl
Ready to cut our own separate paths down the mountain
And meet at the bottom;
Helping each other
Finding friends along the way,
Listening and touching always
All ways.

* * *

### How to Leave Your First, Your Only Home

First, empty all the closets and drawers.
Organize everything into piles to keep, things to sell, possessions to donate.
Telephone all the non-profits you can think of and ask
                                    what they'll come to pick up.
Pack up the picture albums, cigar boxes of photos that hold the life you've lived
                                                                    here.
Disappear during the "estate sale" while your forty-eight years of
                                    accumulation are sold
For pennies.
Be ruthless and throw out everything else.
Every day, walk through the house as it empties,
Remembering.
On the last day, surrender your bedroom to your oldest son.

Walk through the garden; notice the scent of rusting lilacs,
The budding pink rhododendron, white azalea, bleeding hearts, lavender phlox.
Check the herbs: thyme awakening, mint and oregano thriving,
                                                    a few sprouts of parsley
Emerging, chives wild and pungent.
Climb up into the apple tree's crotch:
Note the first growth of rhubarb already gone to seed,
The sagging railroad ties that frame the planting beds.
Straddle, then lie down in the green and white-striped hammock.
Consider digging up one of the Peace roses and some of that slender purple iris.
Reconsider.
Walk the new owners through the house:
Explain the intricacies of appliances, soaking tub, garbage collection, storage
                                                    spaces.
Pack up your few clothes, your travel iron, cosmetics, pills.
In the driveway, hug your next-door neighbors goodbye.
Climb into the car, back out of the driveway.
For a few minutes, gaze at the white house:
*The* deep blue front door
The bed of roses, greening and ready to blossom,
The lush pear tree with its miniscule chartreuse fruit,
One thick cluster of day lilies and all the trees that you kept from oblivion
When this lot was cleared: white pines and maples, ironwood and cherry
Butternut too, with spring's shamrock green grass bordering all.
Exchange a look with your mate
Feel the tears
File away the memories and
Leave.

**Larry Martz**
**Hamilton NJ**

# Everything You Had To Do

*Those boys needed killing. There's no excuse for their behavior. There's no question in your mind. They needed killing worse than any vermin Daddy wanted you to shoot with his old .22 rifle back on the farm. They showed no respect for life. What could they have been thinking to do something so ugly? Their mothers must have abandoned them, if they even had mothers. Two boys drinking beer in a place like that and doing what they did. Must have lost their souls as children. But that's no excuse. And what else could you have done? They needed killing and you had Arthur's shotgun in the trunk and you did what you had to do. When you have to do something, the rest is easy. Just because you're old doesn't mean you're useless. You may not be good for much, but there are still some things you can do. Those boys needed killing and you got it done. Then you did the other thing that had to be done, or you tried to, but that wasn't so easy. Maybe you didn't do that thing right at all.*

Helen's heartbeat thumped in her ears. She stared at the dark stain spreading across the gathered folds of the cotton dress covering her thighs and waited for something to happen. She thought she would feel so different the moment after she did it. She thought she would be in motion somehow, falling away from the earth with that rushing, sinking feeling she remembered from a roller coaster ride taken years ago at an amusement park near the ocean. But nothing like that had happened. Something had gone wrong. She looked up from her lap and waited for things to change, counting her breaths as if they were imaginary sheep jumping over an imaginary fence as her mother had told her to do when Helen was eight years old and afraid of the dark, hoping to fall asleep and hoping to be transported to some better place before she awakened. But her mind was too busy to allow the simple relief of sleep.

*Daddy told you not to think of vermin as living things. Think of them as damage, he used to say. Think of the crows eating the crops and the rats eating the harvest in the barn in winter. Vermin take from us and give nothing back, he'd say. It's us or them. He told you that when you both stood by the woodpile after you had hesitated at the trigger and let a groundhog scramble to his burrow from a clear shot by the tomato garden. Show weakness now, he said, and they'll be the ones with the full bellies, and you and your little brother will be crying from hunger. But brother is gone now, from cancer in his stomach, and so is Daddy gone, long ago after a fall from the barn roof before Arthur married you and took you to the city to work at a factory job. The farm and its lessons seem so far away. And Arthur is gone, too, though only seven months past, late last summer when the third stroke took him. You could see it in his eyes after the second one that he was tired of fighting. The kids came back for a week then, flew in from Florida and New Mexico to make sure you would be all right. But anyone can act all right for a week.*

Helen lowered her eyes again, and in the dim room their focus returned to the stain. She had expected something worse than it looked, or perhaps she was just getting used to the sight.

*You know this whole thing will raise your blood pressure, though Doc Barnes pre-scribed those tiny pills last fall for any kind of upset. But now you can't touch your wrist there to check it. Oh wait, Helen. Don't be such a silly. You get your* pulse *from your wrist, not your pressure.*

Helen looked through the blinds across the small front yard, where a neigh-bor's spotlight pierced a row of sharp-needled pines and lit the cracked driveway. She remembered watching through the years from the same window the concen-tration with which her husband had carefully smoothed an annual layer of black-top sealer each spring.

*A widow like you is half a thing. She sees the work around the house, the mending and the maintenance, the peeling and the wear, but she can't do it all alone. She's too frag-ile or weak or, being used to having a man at her side, never learned the proper way to do things even when she had the strength. And now it's too late for you, Helen. This house would just fall down around you if you stayed here long enough.*

Helen glanced at her lap again, and at her hands clasped together, palms down. The blood on her dress beneath her wrists had started to stiffen as it dried.

*You were only nine when Daddy wanted you to kill a chicken. He said you wouldn't like it, but unpleasant things that had to be done are best done quickly and without thought. He always said too much thinking is for those with too much time. Thought can contract the mind rather than expand it. So you held the chicken on the chopping block and raised the ax and tried not to think, but as your arm dropped you must have thought of something or closed your eyes because the blade missed the chicken's neck and sliced off only the beak, and that bird escaped from your shaking hand and ran around you squawking and splatter-ing blood on your skirt hem as it circled. Remember how Daddy ignored your crying? He just caught that chicken in a flash and killed it without looking at you once, then carried it into the house to the kitchen as if nothing bad had happened.*

Helen looked away from her hands and stood up. She rose slowly, anticipat-ing lightheadedness, but felt only a mild shortness of breath instead. She walked to the bathroom, plugged the drain in the tub, and turned on the hot water. She placed Arthur's shaving case on the blue porcelain rim of the tub.

*You didn't do it right. That's all. You'll have to try another way. And watch what you're doing this time. Don't think, just look. Remember the chicken? But you never killed one. You're getting confused again. Why did those boys have to do that ugly thing? It had been such a pleasant spring afternoon, and you sat on the porch a bit too long after supper, enjoying the smell of blooms in the air, and you drove a little too slowly to the graveyard to water the flowers. Arthur was not a sentimental man. He wasn't tender or loving as he grew older, and certainly not after the strokes. But you took care of him and you would take care of his grave. What else do you have to do, Helen Walters? You care for your dead husband's gravestone flowers and you look out the window. You're not exactly a circus performer, but you don't bother anyone.*

She turned off the hot water, mixed in a little cold to make the plunge bear-able, and swirled the floating bubbles with her fingertips in slow, oval motions. Helen slipped out of her flat shoes. She giggled as she stepped over the rim of the tub and lowered herself into the water, then rested the back of her head against the cool tile to watch her stained dress absorb the warm water and sink below the surface against her skin.

*What a strange way for an old woman to behave. Never mind. Things are different now. It hasn't been a normal day. You drove to the church in the little village outside of Princeton that was once surrounded by corn fields, and you stopped to fill the plastic jug at the old well to water Arthur's flowers, minding your own business as you always do, and then you found those two boys at his grave. It was after dusk, but the sky still held light. You could see them well enough to know what they were doing. You remembered that same posture from when you were a schoolgirl, peeking around a bush near the swimming pond in summer and seeing the boys from school all standing in a row, relieving themselves. What's wrong with the world nowadays? Young men kill each other for sneakers and jackets, and girls have babies as soon as they become women with no plans to marry the fathers. And hoodlums urinate on Arthur's grave, out in the open with a car approaching. Something inside you snapped. You twisted the ignition key and stepped from the driver's door and lifted the trunk lid, knowing what had to be done without a single thought formed in your mind. The shotgun waited under a blanket beneath a piece of cardboard along the Buick's spare tire. Arthur kept it loaded but never fired it. Why did he need a gun in the car anyway? But you knew how to use it.*

Helen unzipped the cover of Arthur's shaving case and removed the straightedge razor. She swiveled the blade from the pivoted hinge of the protective guard and inspected it in the bright light of the overhead bulb.

*He was a man set in his ways, your Arthur. Remember when you bought him that electric shaver for his birthday and he squinted at it as if it were a cup of coffee that an unknowing waitress had sugared without asking? That man used known things that worked, and he thought inventions of convenience were a lazy person's waste of money. Never mind that the electric razor would have made it easier for you to shave him for two years after the strokes began. But those boys were drunk. That was plain enough. They were laughing and talking and paying no attention. It was easy to get close, and you didn't say a word. Just fired two shells and dropped the gun and walked back to the car and drove home. It was a thing that had to be done and it was over with and there's nothing to think about now. You didn't turn around to look. You didn't see where the shots hit. No, Helen. Stop that. Don't do that to yourself. You're starting to think again, and Daddy always said thinking can only mean you have too much time on your hands.*

Helen extended the fingers of her left hand and lowered them below the surface of the water, then cut two deep parallel lines three inches long into her wrist. She winced when the blade first pierced her flesh, but she kept her eyes open and repeated the process farther up her forearm. When she released the razor, it sank in zigzag motions through the colored currents in the tub.

You did it right this time. Sitting in the dark in the living room by the window and barely breaking the skin with that dull paring knife was not the way to go. You closed your eyes then, too. This time was better. You could see what you had to do. The light is good in here, and the warm water feels soothing. It's been a long time since you've soaked in this tub. It helps to be tired. And you can rest now. Everything you had to do is done.

# Fire Dancer

Norman and I looked and looked for ashes or footprints in that part of the pasture , but we never did find any. I'll tell you all about it . . . .

In my summer world, vacation from country school was a time of adventure, exploration, and barefoot, shirtless days. Great white oak and red oak trees, soft and hard maples, hickories, elms, and basswoods dominated one corner of the farm. It was a quiet, mystical place. By treading very softly and quietly, you could see a red squirrel walking a tightrope out to the end of a limb, then jumping to a branch on an adjacent tree or you might spy a busier one on the woodlot floor, burying an acorn which would serve as a snack next winter.

Sometimes a large black crow would interrupt my careful stalking with a loud "Caw! Caw! Caw!" Now all the creatures in my forest would scurry for cover and the game would be over, for a while at least.

There were ravines which ran through the farm. They were quiet places, too, where the excitement of exploration made my heart beat faster and harder, so that I could feel it.

These mini-valleys were bordered with osage orange trees which produced "hedge apples." On the ground, there would be many of the hard, round, heavy, lime colored balls about the size of a large orange. They were inedible except that cattle might chew on them. For me, they were a wonder to see and examine, but only good for throwing.

The hedge rows would grow to a considerable height, and this living fence was impenetrable for anything larger than a rabbit. One couldn't even see through this wall of vegetation, so the ravines were as private and secluded as my upstairs bedroom in the big farmhouse.

The shaded margins of the ravines and the big brush piles provided excellent hiding places for rabbits and quail. A few years later, ring necked pheasants found this to be a good stopping place. I could always frighten a rabbit or a covey of quail into rapid departure as I worked my way down through these places. They would return time after time, as though they enjoyed the game.

Small, clear streams chuckled their way down through the centers of these little valleys, and thick bluegrass turf, soggy and damp near the creeks, covered the ground to where the hedges separated my private worlds from the cultivated fields on the outside. Frogs and their tadpoles, along with crayfish and a myriad of water bugs, inhabited the pools along the creeks. I constructed earthen dams on my rivers, with spillways and with roads across the tops of the dams. I named one big frog "Jumpy" and was glad to see he was still there on a day after a hard rain washed away most of the dam where he hung out.

There came a time when I could guide a friend to every groundhog den, rabbit hole, hollow tree, squirrel's nest, or spring in my summer world. Of course, there was the hayloft in the old barn to play in on a rainy day, the hard maple tree to climb in the front yard, the Concord grapes on the vines out by the garden, and

"Babe," my beautiful bay mare. I could tell an entire story just about her.

But I want to tell you about my Uncle Bill and a most unusual summer night out by one of the ravines a night and a place I will never forget . . . .

My Uncle Bill had a parrot and was quite a story teller, quite a reader, very well informed for the times. He was a bachelor until he married a widow lady who I can dimly remember. Both were near seventy when the wedding took place, and you can understand why the entire neighborhood was excited. People up and down our road were mostly Quakers. Many of them knew he had studied much about Darwin's theory of evolution and believed it. He was not a member of their church. Even so, they crowded around Bill's house late one evening, banging on pots and pans (an event called a charivari or shivaree) and yelling for treats.

To this day I still ponder about one of Bill's stories and related events which sent chills up and down my spine . . . and still do sometimes. The happenings also scared the dickens out of my real good friend, Norman Foster, who lived in the farm house across a small field from our place.

It was in late September, 1928. Norman and I were both ten and we had spent much of the summer exploring and playing together. His house was near enough to ours that we could yell and make each other hear. One of the things we talked about but hadn't accomplished that summer was to camp out all night. Many kids of that time liked to imagine they were explorers or pioneers or cowboys living out in the wilds, watching out for mountain lions and things. We decided, on a warm September day, that we'd like to roll up some blankets (we didn't have sleeping bags back then) and some provisions, also matches and a hatchet for making a nice camp fire, and proceed to sleep out all night. We would make our camp someplace out on the back end of the farm where we'd really be away from civilization.

We asked our folks for permission, and it was given. We could do it the next evening. That would be on Saturday night and would be best because school had started. Dad wanted to know the location of our campsite, and we discussed this at supper when Uncle Bill was there as a guest.

Bill was quiet as the folks and I discussed our plan. I indicated we would make our camp on the knoll on the west side of the second creek, where the large osage orange hedgerow would be at our backs. We would be able to look down on the creek and the ravine, and across to the pasture about a city block to the east.

My uncle finally cleared his throat and spoke up. I sensed that another tall tale might be coming.

Bill's tone was very serious. He glanced out the window (it was dark outside) and spoke in a deliberate, confidential manner. "You all realize this is Indian Summer, don't you?" He paused, saying no more while we waited for him to go on. But he just looked down at his plate, then raised his eyebrows and shrugged.

I looked at Mom and Dad, and they were both busy chewing their food, not looking inquisitive or anything, and just thinking their own thoughts. My curiosity finally got the best of me, and I asked, "What about Indian Summer, Uncle Bill?"

His eyes remained lowered. After a long pause and a drink from his water glass, he said, "The dancers."

By now I was really getting up on the edge of my chair and I asked, "What dancers?"

Bill raised his eyes to mine and then looked at Dad as if to get his permission to say more. Dad looked serious but nodded, and Bill leaned back in his chair and spoke in a low tone. "Well, you know, this was all Indian territory around here about the time my dad came here." He went on, "You saw the arrow heads we found just about where you're going to hunker down tomorrow night, so you can be sure this was their home, and they loved it and all that. They probably camped right where you're going to."

Bill was good at making things sound dramatic, so I wasn't really surprised when he paused again, looked at the window, and spoke in even lower tones. "Well, I never saw it myself, but lots of the older people in this area have said the reason they call this Indian Summer is that along about now, on cool nights, when there isn't a breeze blowing or a bird chirping, and when all you can hear out in some out-of-the-way place is maybe a frog or a cricket, the spirits might come out. Some say they saw them." He took another drink from his glass, moved his chair back and murmured, "My! It's getting late, and this old bird better back to his place, feed the parrot, and get ready for bed."

"Bill, what did they see?" I wanted to hear more, but I tried not to act too excited about this.

"Oh, I've heard different accounts, but some say the ghosts of the dead Indians were doing some kind of a dance around a fire, in a place they loved. Then they just faded away. Next morning when it wasn't so scary, witnesses would go out there and look around, but they'd never find anything."

My imagination was working and I think my heart beat a little faster, but my reason told me that Uncle Bill was pulling my leg. While it wasn't very kind of me, I blurted out, "Aw, I don't believe it. That's just one of your tall tales."

Bill paused at the door, gave sort of an apologetic little smile and said, "I guess I might believe it if I saw it myself, but I always thought it was just a story somebody hatched up for the fun of it." Then he went out into the night. His comment surprised me.

Mom shamed me with, "I hope you didn't hurt your Uncle's feelings, Richard." I felt a bit sorry about my remark for most of that evening but had forgotten about it by the next day. Norm and I got busy gathering our things together. Saturday was still a warm day and it looked like we would be camping out.

In the middle of the afternoon we went back to the second ravine, kicking out a couple rabbits on the way, stopping to repair one of my dams, and trying to identify old Jumpy. For a while we pretended we were Tom Sawyer and Huckleberry Finn, but decided it would be more fun to be two explorers—mountain men going into strange, wild territory. This became easier to imagine when the sun started to go down and light faded.

We went up onto the knoll where we'd placed our blankets and some sandwiches Mom had made, not even thinking about the fact that tough old mountain men didn't have Mom around to make sandwiches for them. We made up our beds, finding it surprisingly hard to eliminate all the hard lumps that you could feel under them. The sun set, we built a fire, darkness descended, the air became cooler and a bit damp, stars came out, and we could finally see the big dipper. The frogs down below started to croak, and the crickets chirped.

Then I remembered Bill's "Indian Summer when it's real quiet in out-of-the-way places." Suddenly, I realized I hadn't told Norm that story. It was really very dark now, the air felt quite chilly, and we had stopped talking a while ago. The stars, the night sounds, and our imaginations had cast a kind of spell. I was alert, listening for any strange sound, and hunkered down very near our campfire. I was about to repeat Bill's tall tale when Norm jumped up, pointed to the pasture across the ravine, and yelled, "My gosh! What's that?"

I looked and saw a fire over there. Not only that, but we could see a figure hopping and dancing in a circle around the blaze. This only lasted for about a half minute, and then the fire flared up to a good big size but quickly died down and was gone. The night seemed darker than ever.

Both Norm and I were frozen in place for a few seconds and we squinted intently into the darkness across the ravine. We listened for the sounds of any persons or things out there, but there was nothing.

"What the heck was that?" Norm's voice was shaky as he came and stood close to me.

By now my heart was starting to beat normally again and I wasn't sure, but I thought maybe I knew what had happened. I figured that Uncle Bill had decided to put some frosting on the cake he had served up for me on the preceding evening —some added excitement in the tale he'd spun. Then I decided, craftily, to use the tall tale myself. I began the story with Norm's eyes staring out from the blanket which he had shrunk down into.

"Well, you know this is Indian Summer, don't you? Some people say the spirits of the dead Indians, who really loved this land, sometimes come to out-of-the-way places on September nights when things are quiet." I said this in a very low, dramatic tone —like Uncle Bill. "Then the witnesses usually see them doing a dance around a fire. The next day, when it's not so scary, the people go out there and look for ashes and footprints and things."

"Gosh! Do you believe it?" Norm pulled his blanket clear up over his head and turned his back to the fire so he could look out into the darkness around us.

"Well, I sure never believed it until tonight. It's different when you really see it." I was trying to act cool, but was pretty scared myself. Was it really Bill over there? Now Norm moved even closer to me. I wrapped up in my own blanket and soon heard him putting more wood on the fire so it would blaze up higher. It took me an awfully long time to doze off, and maybe Norm didn't sleep at all because he didn't let the fire die down much until the sun was peaking over the horizon. We rolled up our blankets and things for an early trip home and a good breakfast. We'd come back to search the pasture.

Later, I told Uncle Bill we had seen the Indian spirits. I was fishing for some kind of reaction but he just looked skeptical and said, "I think you're pulling my leg. As I told you, I'd never believe it unless I saw it myself. You must have been dreaming." He acted like he just wasn't interested and went on out to the corn crib to get feed for the pigs. I was really frustrated except for knowing that I had really pulled a good one on Norman.

One thing puzzles me though, and this is true. Norm and I searched and searched out in that pasture and never did find anything. There weren't any ashes or foot prints or other signs. To this day I can't figure out how Bill built a fire and hopped around out there without leaving some evidence. Sometimes I get to thinking that maybe I was dreaming. But I know I wasn't! And there should have been ashes, or some singed grass, or feathers, or something. . . .

*Margaret Bobalek King*
*East Derry, NH*

## Prospect In Brown

I walk through the cemetery on top of the hill
where sun catches the sheen of fallen leaves
horseback brown, churning beneath
my playful feet or dangling a spire's height
above me on rough, gray branches. A little breeze
tears holes in their fine fabric, but some hang on.

Chocolate brown, warm golden brown,
Autumn brown, all around; Oak leaf brown
on the ground or towering above squirrel's home,
they fly over my head. Spinning on stems,
they fall and die like brown-clad soldiers
crashing down on the sands at Normandy.

Rattling in the wind, the ones who stay
seem to say, "We linger into deep November."
Across the path shakes an answer. "Or even
into the cold of sap-cracking season." I wait
by hardwood Maple, my place of peace among
the trees in seasons either of heat or of freezing.

My month is brown, my birthday brown,
a lit-up crayon-box like the trees I love
when they shed their leaves and I can go
crunch-crunch like a child again, a happy child!
Let me take a bite, chocolate Autumn,
Let me taste you in one whole chunk!

## Sherry Robertson
## Palm Coast FL

### Death, Where Is Your Victory?

I feel you coming.
As if I could almost smell you.
It was a few years back that I became ever so aware of your persistent calling.
Making believe I am not home while you are ringing the doorbell to pick me up for dinner is no use,
You can see through the closed door.
The locked window holds you back no more.

You are there and yet, I know not the time dinner will be served.
Although I know that the food will be the best meal I have ever eaten,
I still long to wait as the hunger grows.
A little while longer to sort out the top from the bottom.
Soaking in the joys with which I have been blessed.
Trying to grow in letting go of small annoyances and short sufferings and giving them no glory.
While I gain pleasure in watching the seeds He has watered grow and mature.

Knowing that in a short time you will bring me to a banquet where there will be no tears or sorrow.
You think you are stealing something from me but you do not hold the keys to Heaven or Hell.
Where flying without an aircraft makes no sense to the earthly mind.
You come to take my breath away,
But as soon as you do I will be with Him.
It will be glorious,
No shortness in it.

Back and forth I go,
Begging for release from the vessel that holds me here,
And the struggle to ward off fiery arrows,
To begging for the sight of evidence of birth in those I have borne.
Hiking through the mountains one more time,
Gatlinburg at Christmas,
Hand dipped foot long hot dogs and funnel cakes,
A foot stomping bluegrass song about your enemy.

No it does not appear you will win this day,
For what is winning when you lose either way?

## Ina Prieditis
## Minneapolis MN

## Quotations....................

Quotations are other men's flowers
often soaked
in a vibrant paint.......
They can be
a scene
to which
a thought
IS
added in
where one's complaints
seem hibernate
and slicing words
are thrown away....
thus
the quotes
bloom like flowers....
*n'est pas*

*William Beyer*
*Belvidere, IL*

## Tornado

First sighted. at 2:47
this early April afternoon,
the tornado,
an unpredicted intruder,
moves rapidly;
hinting chaos .

Sky
is midnight-black.

A sudden mood
of panic
lingers;
suggests immediate danger.

I advance
from indefinite shape
of barn,
unfinished chores,
toward farmhouse,
safety of cellar door,
with increased concern,
move through continual wall
of dust;
hear the close,
relentless voice
of a desperate wind.

**Sandra D. Thibault**
**Londonderry NH**

## The Graveyard

*A* cold, brittle wind
Travels through
The graveyard
Ruffling *petals*
On the flowers *laid*
*Atop* the *box*
Holding my *baby.*
*Each* day lasts a year
*Since his* death
My heart not *knowing*
Where to find my heart
*I* am enveloped *in* grief.
*Hot,* acrid tears fall
*Forming* twin rivers
Down the *sides* of my face.
Desire to *live* has left my body
There *is nothing* left to *give.*
My life *will be* planted
With my baby.

*Melanie Florence*
*Fairfax, VA*

# Into the Blue

Over the past few years, I've been turning increasingly green. It varies: sometimes I'm greener than a dollar bill and other times I'm the color of a scarcely ripe peach. Just a tinge of green, but green nevertheless.

I've figured it out; my level of greenness depends directly upon my level of anxiety. I won't say I'm a cowardly person but every day I have to encourage myself with the chant from "The Little Engine That Could" before I will get out of bed, open the front door, answer the phone, collect the mail or leave the house. I think I can, I think I can.

I've given up gardening completely. Too much green. And driving? Don't even mention it. Or crowds of any type. Or caffeine. They all accentuate the green.

I think all the pine trees surrounding our little town initiated my color change. They outnumber the people here at least a million to one. And they're multiplying. Every fall, when the trees release their greenish-yellow pollen and powder the town, I feel myself turning a richer shade of green.

But it's more than that. My greenness has come to surge and retreat constantly, not just seasonally. So I've come to the conclusion that the pine trees release oxygen with little bitty pieces of chlorophyll attached to it. When I breathe it in, the chlorophyll sticks to my lungs and stays there. Everyone else breathes it out, but for me it sticks and turns me green.

I think this greenness also comes from within my own body, possibly my gall bladder. I have a colicky stomach and whenever I'm required to go into town, I throw up first. Aren't occasional pain and vomit classic gall bladder symptoms? And isn't bile green? I figure that it's building up and, with nowhere else to go, it seeps into my skin, turning it green.

Because of my green problem, I've taken to staying at home as much as I can. But if I must go out, I first cake my face with coverup makeup and put on a dark turtleneck with long sleeves and slacks, even in warm weather. Sometimes I even wear gloves. But still, I think the green color leaks through. Otherwise, why do people always look startled when they see me and then ask pseudo-innocent questions like, "Hi Julie. I haven't seen you in ages. What have you been doing with yourself?

My husband, Ted, does not agree that I'm turning green. Although I've spent days and nights explaining it to him, he continuously argues with me. So I decided to stop discussing it. In fact, I haven't talked about it for at least two weeks. And I think he concludes that if I don't mention it, the problem has gone away. Only it hasn't.

But right now our conflict doesn't matter. In one week we're going to California, just the three of us, during the brown part of the year. We'll be meeting my wheelchair-bound brother, Greg, his wife, and their two children at Clear Lake. Greg has rented two condos, the bottom floor for his family and the top floor for ours. Oh, I'm certain that I'll be comfortable there. Not only materially comfortable but atmospherically comfortable. I'll get out of green into brown.

The big day finally arrives, a Saturday in late July. Ted drives, our teenage son, Josh, hunches over his Game Boy in the back seat immersed in headphone heaven, and I try, again, to talk to Ted about my greenness. But he shuts me out and stares at the road, pressing his lips together in disapproval. So I sigh and hold it in for rest of the nine-hour drive. But I can feel my greenness building up. I just know I'm going to be as green as a jalapeno pepper when we get there.

Our two-story condo sits directly on the lake and we park next to the rows of red, blue and yellow flags that welcome us in. Primary colors. As they whip in the breeze, flinging off their reds and blues and yellows, I feel the warm colors through my shirt. Outside the car, I pull up my sleeve and study my arm. Yes, the green buildup from the long drive is already beginning to dissipate.

As I knock on the door, I'm jittery with anticipation. I want to talk to Greg about my greenness. I know he'll understand. After all, Greg can be a bit green himself. But an unknown young girl flings open the door and looks up at me, flabbergasted. I stare back, nodding understandingly. She has probably never seen a green person before.

"I'm sorry," I say. "I must have the wrong unit." Then I glance at the note in my hand and the number on the door. They match.

A second later I hear Greg call out,"Julie, is that you?" He quickly wheels past the girl and I see a wide grin on his face. "Oh, it's so good to see you. How was the drive?"

I stand there for a moment, perplexed. Who is this extra child?

After I recover, I greet him while looking over his head. Three unknown adults and an unknown baby, in addition to this unknown girl, are sitting around a long dining room table in an open, all-purpose room. From their surprised expressions, I know that they can see my greenness. My stomach lurches but they nod politely and wave a hello and I tell myself that my dear, sweet brother must have warned them.

Ted, Josh and I enter the condo as Cindy, Greg's wife, walks around the kitchen counter, wiping her hands on her apron. At the same time, my two nephews emerge from one of the bedrooms and run up to hug my legs. "Hi Aunt Julie!" they say.

Then come the introductions: Kemper, Joan and her husband Terry, their baby and their little girl. "I didn't want to drive all the way out here by myself," Cindy apologizes, "so I invited Joan and Terry along to help with the drive. And Kemper is Terry's brother. He lives in San Francisco and came up here to stay for the weekend. Isn't that nice? By the way, I gave them the extra bedroom in your unit. I hope you don't mind."

I feel sick. Not only my skin, but now my insides, are burning. I know my face must be as green as it possibly can get. But I try to be polite. "Hello, everyone," I say, covering my flaming cheeks with my hands. "It's so nice to meet you. It was a long drive, though, and as you can see, my greenness is flaring up."

Greg, Cindy, Kemper, Terry, Joan; they all stare at me as if I've grown a third eye.

"I'm terribly sorry," I continue. "I think I'll just go upstairs and wash my face." I quickly turn and escape out of the condo to our car.

Ted is close behind me. "What is the matter with you?" he says as he pulls out a suitcase.

In our bedroom I try to explain to Ted how my body is filling up with green. I rock on the bed with the pain of it.

His face is weighed down with concern; eyebrows down, outside eye edges down, nose down, mouth down, lines on his face down, chin dimpled with the support of it all.

"I thought it would only be family," I say and begin to cry.

He takes my wet hand away from my face and pats it. "It's okay, Julie. These people seem nice. You can handle it; I know you can."

After I compose myself, we go downstairs. But when we enter Greg's condo for the second time, I am hit with people, too many people. Is it my imagination or is the room even more crowded?

I see Cindy come in through the sliding glass door accompanied by a gray-green barbeque cloud, holding a platter heaped with steaks. Behind her, sitting on the back porch, are the distressing newcomers: an annoying childhood acquaintance, Tammy, and her bratty teenage daughter.

What are they doing here? I glance at Cindy again. She is staring at me with narrow eyes and a twisted mouth. A demeanor of evil.

Around the dining room table sit Tammy's weird ex-husband in his goofy hat, Greg catty-corner in his wheelchair, and Kemper and Terry facing each other, all talking, all drinking beer in green bottles. To my right, Ted is pulling a beer out of the cooler and Josh is piling a plate with green-tinged chips. Beyond the table, my two nephews play "Bop-it" in a back corner while Joan nurses the baby on the couch, bouncing in time with her daughter as she hops up and down, up and down next to her, yelling the Humpty Dumpty nursery rhyme at the top of her lungs.

Green sound waves reflect around and around the room, amplifying and mixing with a thick green swirl of beer-permeated air. I feel woozy.

"Come on in, Julie," Greg calls out cheerily above the din. "Get yourself a beer."

Cindy smiles, a malicious green smile. "Yeah, Julie. Join the crowd."

I take a step in and try to inhale. But there's no oxygen in here. I'm suffocating. My stomach is in knots, my chlorophyll-laden lungs are crying for relief.

"I need some fresh air," I pant. "I think I'll walk to the lake."

"Okay," Greg says. "But don't take too long. We might run out of food." He laughs and dips down to sip on a green straw in his beer.

I weave through people to the sliding glass door, pass by Tammy and her daughter on the porch, and aim toward the not-too-distant vision of shimmering blue. I cross the lawn quickly so that the green won't absorb through my shoes and crunch over a tan gravel path to the solid dark brown dock. Then I walk to the end, clutch the hot wooden railing and lean forward on it.

Blue lake surrounds me, brown supports me. I fan myself, breathing in deeply. Breathing in soothing blue and sympathetic brown. But with that breath something flies into my mouth, causing me to cough. What is it?

I focus on the air. It's thick with flies. Minuscule green flies. I feel a stirring beneath my hand and quickly remove it. Long, green insects are crawling on the brown rail, in mass movement, like locusts demolishing a crop. Solid brown transforms into quivering green. I look down. Beneath the rail, wispy spider webs are filled with convulsing green bugs, ruled over by huge green spiders. I step back and almost slip on a dock covered with squirming green worms.

I stretch out my hands. They're overrun with masses of undulating green. Insects are crawling into my nose, my ears, my eyes; they're creeping up my legs and burrowing into my skin, turning me green, green through and through. I brush at my arms, my legs, my face. But it's too late.

I lower my gaze to the clear, sparkling lake and I know. I must plunge into the blue. I must cleanse myself of green by surrounding myself, inside and out, with pure, elemental blue.

**Mike Robinson**
**Los Angeles CA**

# High Stakes

If Thursday night had been any busier, Joe Mullard probably wouldn't have noticed the two guys that took the corner pool table. They were professionals, tried and true, their suits groomed and pressed with an ironing of success. What Joe didn't understand was what the hell they were doing walking into Abe's Corner Bar in the first place.

"Can I getcha fellas anything?"

His voice cut the ribbon of their conversation. They looked back at Joe, smiling almost patronizingly.

"Do I want anything?" one of the men mused half-rhetorically. "I'm not sure. This place always brings the alcoholic out of me."

"You're not kiddin', doofus," said his friend. The twinkling glints in their eyes, a subtle hint of a close connection, made Joe think they were gay, and immediately trailing that thought was an image of them locked in a passionate horizontal embrace on the pool table. The redneck conservative in him surged with disgust, knowing that, with Castro Street several blocks over, the scenario was far from impossible.

"The last time I was drunk here I had a kid," the first man said. "She was married, too. I got the hell outta there for a while."

"Well," countered the other. "I wouldn't say that necessarily."

"True, you certainly had a fuckin' field day with that one."

"You sure you guys don't want anything?" Joe asked. His face was lop-sided in quizzicality. Part of him felt like he was the butt of some Candid Camera joke.

"No, thank you, we're fine."

"Okay, boys."

One of the men sauntered off to claim the corner table. The other began to follow then hesitated with a thought. He leaned over, casually resting his elbow on the counter like a sleazy executive about to rub his fingers together in a 'I can make it worth your while' gesture.

"Mr. Mullard."

Joe's ears perked up. At the moment, the fact that this well-kempt businessman knew his name wasn't weird. It quirkily made sense.

"You can put your worries to rest about your niece," he assured Joe. "I've been polishing my billiards ability."

"Excuse me?"

He knocked on the wooden counter, as though for good luck. The man joined his friend in the corner, who was busy shuffling the triangle of billiard balls into breaking position. He obsessed over it, refining, tweaking, a person who needs and has control.

Joe let the topic go, reassuring himself that maybe the man was a friend of Jasmine's, or a close enough acquaintance to his niece that he knew of her vehicle's crippling brush with a drunk-driving Harold Robeson, a regular at Abe's whose full bladder Joe was ironically responsible for that night.

"Ready for a beat down?" the second man said with playful malice.

"Name the stakes, bitch boy," came the equally playful reply.

Joe kept one ear on them as they gave the tips of their cues noogies with blocks of chalk. Frat boy rivalry came out of their mouths, packaged in an innately business-like tone. The combination was jarring and bizarre.

"Okay, we'll play the pockets then," announced the first man. "Three pockets for Salvation, three for Damnation."

"Good, the classic. You wanna break?"

Abe's Corner Bar was getting busier, filling with the usual two kinds of people. Young bar hoppers were lapped up and spat right back out, while the regulars, the guy-guys, their stomachs all looking as though they had swallowed three volleyballs, nestled in for a night of lifting, guzzling and pissing.

There was a harsh smack and clatter of billiard balls. The first man had broken.

"Nothing in," observed his friend teasingly. "Now watch how it's done."

The second man took aim and pounded the nine ball into the far corner pocket. He stood back, broadcasting his pride with a loud and bright smile. The first man pinched the bridge of his nose, perhaps feeling the dawn of a headache.

"Worlds or Souls?" he sighed obligatorily.

"Hmmm," mulled the second man. "I'm feeling personal tonight. Let's play Souls."

Abe's was swelling at an unusual pace for a Thursday, although, to many, Thursday was close enough to the weekend to warrant a night on the town. Bobby had started his shift already, taking some of the load off Joe's shoulders. A valley of people surrounded him now. They painted the air with alcohol breath, temporarily forgetting there was a world outside the filled glasses and curvy bottles. Joe had a strange feeling that he was at the center of everything, that this dingy little San Francisco bar was the bullseye in the perfect circle of the world, the universe. People of all shades, sizes and colors entered with looks of accepted comfort on their faces, as if knowing this was the place to be, and Joe thought of the tavern being used as some inverted, contemporary Noah's Ark. He chuckled.

He felt steady eyes on him all of a sudden, and knew where from. Joe peered over in the direction of the two suits, both of whom orbited a chaotic solar system of balls in green velvet space. One man squinted and analyzed a possible shot as he smothered his cue's tip with more chalk.

The first man, however, the one who had spoken to Joe about his niece, looked towards him and winked knowingly. He assumed the position, determined, sharply eyeing the ball at the end of the cue. His tongue poked its way into the musty light, flattened against his upper lip in solemn concentration.

"The soul of Jasmine Mullard," he said. "In the corner Salvation pocket."

One sharp jab later, the cue ball glanced off the striped ten ball, sending it into a rapid sunset below the rim of the pocket.

"Nothin' but net," the man beamed. "Eat that, cockass."

The second man smirked and shook his head, as though he'd just heard a painfully bad joke. "Such language. You know virtually everyone here still thinks they're offending you when a curse word passes their lips."

"Let 'em think what they want. If they actually think I'd stoop to their level and torture or fry them for a fucking word, let them waste their lives pissing in their pants."

"Yeah, since that's supposedly my job," the second man winked. He nodded towards the table. "Albert Gershwin, middle Damnation pocket."

The phone rang twice before Joe heard it. He finished pouring a vodka cranberry for a lovely petite blonde, who gave him a thin, disinterested smile. His own face was returning the smile until the phone reached his ear, the grim news following soon thereafter.

"Joe?" came a blubbering female voice.

"Mom?" His eyes grew in size. She seldom called him at work, usually complaining that she could never hear him over the rugged purr of the bar crowds. "What's wrong? What is it?"

"It's Jazzy," Denise Mullard said. "She just slipped away from us. I...I don't understand, she was doing so much better..."

*Oh God*, Joe thought, then whispered it aloud. A million candles flared between his breasts. From the darkened pool table, the first man glanced in his direction apologetically.

Oh God Oh God Oh God No what have I done?

"....I was holding her hand at the time..." his mother cried distantly. Transfixed in shock, Joe slipped the receiver back into its cradle and stared blankly at someone's quarter-empty beer glass.

"Bobby?" he tried to say with the least emotional crack in his voice.

"Yeah, Joe?"

"I'm gonna, um, step outside for a smoke. I'll be right back."

Bobby, in the midst of pouring water for a woman (the petite blonde, in fact), nodded his head and gave a thumbs-up with his free hand. Joe was envious of the boy, who had just popped out of Bartending School and had so much before him. Abe's Corner was just a pit stop for him as he eagerly rolled on through life. Yet Joe also knew that life wouldn't ignore Bobby, as it never let anyone off the hook youth was just wet cement, not yet hardened and unconsciously awaiting the inevitable vandal.

The Bay Area air slapped his entire body with a cold palm, like a paranoid wife to an adulterous husband. It was refreshing, and much needed after the phone call.

*Jasmine is dead.*

Sucking the noxious spirit of the cigarette down did not help as much as he thought it would. The cancer-stick ate itself within a good five minutes, and by the time it met with the ground and subsequently the bottom of his shoe, Joe Mullard felt more empty than ever.

Jasmine, the closest you've ever come to a daughter, is dead. And she won't be coming back. You know why, Mr. Mullard?

He headed back towards the door, holding it open for two ladies who were sure to leave after getting an eyeful of the tavern's interior. He followed them in.

There was another billiard ball smack.

The suits' pool game was almost finished; the eight ball lay solitary in the middle of the table now, a wayward eye throwing a sightless gaze at the ceiling. The two men stood holding their cues with imperial authority, much in the manner of staff-toting palace guards.

"Your shot," said the first man, adding jokingly, "No pressure."

Joe's chest began to curl unto itself, folding and twisting into a hot breathless knot. He kept seeing Jasmine: Jasmine as a grade-schooler, eagerly trying to tag along with he and his buddies; Jasmine as a strikingly beautiful teenager; Jasmine trying to decide between tears and joyful shouts as she packed for her freshman year at Colorado State. He couldn't believe she was gone, and it was all because of him, *all* because of him, the morbid irony of letting Harry-fucking-Robeson feign sobriety and get away with it, letting his inebriated hands grasp a wheel and steer Jasmine Mullard's life into a rapid and miserable twilight.

A large gag of disgust and self-loathing coalesced in his throat. Feeling like a gutted fish, Joe began feeling for something in the space of the cupboards below. His hands hopped like eager frogs over Lost & Found bins, recycle boxes and other miscellaneous crap, until finally landing on the desired object, tucked shamefully in the very back behind three empty Jack Daniels bottles.

There was another clattering smack of billiard balls, this time from the other table. Several guys had started up a game.

Joe cautiously retrieved the gun which was wrapped in a tattered green towel that had never seen the inside of a washer or dryer and carried it like a dirty diaper towards the bathroom. Once inside, he waited until one of the pot-bellied regulars had finished at the urinal before unraveling the towel.

Out on the tavern floor, the second man smugly claimed, "This one's for our gracious bartender."

He leaned down and readied his eight ball shot.

"Damnation, corner pocket."

*Barbara Smith*
*Philippi, WV*

# Lucky Number Seven

Tomorrow he would stand on the seventh tee with Ron and Bill and Marty, and too-fat Ron would say, "Hey, Lester, we're sorry about your wife. You have the honors." It would be true. The three friends would be sorry about Miriam's death, and he, Lester, would have the honors, for at forty-three years of age and in top physical condition, he had become an excellent golfer. He could beat them all.

On second thought, it might be better to hold off for a while. He had better not break par tomorrow. He would play klutz a while longer. They would buy it, for he had a reputation for being inconsistent, sometimes wild, especially on his drives.

Today he must be very careful. He must stand here in the funeral parlor being mournful, perhaps a little tearful, while the floral pieces were being delivered and tiered around Miriam's casket, while the music soothed his supposedly ragged nerves, while friends and strange neighbors paid curious respect, while the services were performed and the coffin was buried. Today he must be the bereaved husband, the remorseful perpetrator of the fatal accident, the guilty party wearing a dark blue suit.

He was far more guilty than anyone imagined. He had actually murdered his wife.

It had taken him seven years, though he had lost count of precisely when he had first thought of it. He and Miriam had had some good years knowing that they needed each other, knowing that in their homely, predictable ways, they made a perfect pair. There had never been love, but they had both pretended. There had never been children either. That they could not pretend. Both of them had been, unfortunately, far too intelligent not to become bored.

Lester was even more intelligent than his well-read wife, he knew, and so he had been planning her murder for years. At first it had been day-dreaming, a game, figuring out what might or might not work, figuring out what she might herself be planning.

Lester for years had really been hoping that Miriam would try to kill him. Then, if he lived, he could plead self-defense. He knew she had been thinking about it. Sometimes he had caught her slumped in her favorite ragged brown chair, browsing through accounts of old murders, undoubtedly measuring the possible success of various and sundry methods. Sometimes he had seen her look up from her knitting, and he knew she was calculating his strength. According to clues she had left around, she first considered poisoning, then a hyperallergenic reaction brought on by an overdose of the serum which he kept in the refrigerator and which she administered to him when he started sneezing and wheezing. Then it was strangling, then a fall from their roof—and he actually had fallen while adjusting the bathroom vent which had mysteriously gotten bent. He had slipped on a loose shingle which had somehow been laid on top of those firmly attached to the roof. Fortunately, he had suffered merely one broken one arm and two sprained toes. He had to admit now, as he smoothed back his thin, graying hair, that he didn't know what she had been thinking of lately.

Obviously, it didn't matter. It had taken him a while, but he had finally beaten her to it.

He had enjoyed every minute of the planning of her demise. Unlike his obviously unstable wife, Lester had had only one plan, start to finish. But even while he was planning the method, he had paid special attention, reverent attention, to the superstition that had governed his life. Seven.

He had waited seven years and six and a half months, and he had practiced seven days of every week, even when it rained.

In all of the twenty-seven years of their marriage, Lester and Miriam had had one very important point in common. They had both loved golf. They had played together at least once a week, though they had played apart far more often. Miriam had taken on a variety of opponents, but Lester had stuck to the same cronies—Ron and Bill and Marty, who at yesterday's inquest had testified to his erratic game and, of course, to his sterling character. Today they would be three of the pallbearers.

Lester would have liked more challenge, more honest-to-God competition. He was a better golfer than the other three. However, they had never really known it. They knew that his short game, the chipping, the putts, was almost letter-perfect. They knew that his irons, even the long ones, never shanked, never worm-burned, never faltered. He might, they observed, miss an occasional three-wood. The weak spot in his game, however, was his drive. Perhaps in a round of eighteen holes, half of his drives would be faultless—down the middle, straight as an arrow, and longer than any of his opponents'. But the other half were disasters. There were no words for his wildness. Some shots took off with an incredible hook, some with a slice, and some lofted so high as to be termed star-kissers.

"It's sad," Ron would say, hitching his trousers up under his belly. "I wish to God you could correct that. If you'd only get that drive under control, you be playing scratch. My god, you could go on the tour. But that drive!"

Lester would fight the impulse to laugh. He would smile instead at Marty and Bill. No one but God and he would ever know that his wildness was deliberate. And Lester was sure that God would forgive him, for God knew what a colossal bore Miriam was.

His inconsistency was, indeed, determined, for Lester had practiced behind his barn, practiced particularly his woods, hour after hour after tedious hour, hitting out balls and shagging them, shifting his stance, perfecting his grip until he was more than professional. Finally, indeed, Lester was sure he could hit any target. Not only that, but if that target was within a hundred yards, he could guarantee a bullseye. And he could do it from various angles, not unlike Scotty Pippin doing the four corners.

At long last it was time. The conditions were absolutely perfect. Miriam had spent two rainy days boring him right out of his mind. She and his visiting mother-in-law had chattered him right up the walls, discussing menus and quilt squares and home permanents. Then his purple-haired mother-in-law had gone home to Bridgeport, and they had been alone, and when he made a half-hearted pass at Miriam, she had responded as usual—she wanted to finish the laundry. "But tomorrow's Saturday," she had reasoned. "How about getting up early for a little golf?" She had actually smiled as she made the suggestion. They could get in eighteen holes before lunch, and then he would still have time to clean the garage.

"Perfect," he had smiled back, and he had gone to bed and slept like the innocent. Saturday—the seventh day of the week. And it was July, the seventh month!

He waited until the seventh hole, for conditions there were just what he wanted. The women's tee was ahead of the men's but off at an angle. Miriam had trusted Lester's skill, for his aim on this hole had always been perfect. He had yet to miss a single drive—at least when she was with him—so she had patiently waited right on her own grassy tee. Stoop-shouldered, she waited. After his ball had sailed straight and true over the hill, she, too, would execute a beautiful drive. She was a fine golfer also, but she never knew how truly fine Lester was.

The sky had been clear, the sun shining, and the course was full of players. Lester stepped onto the well-worn tee, found a flat spot near the marker, and pushed the small peg into the turf. He placed his Top-Flite upon it. Then he straightened, checked Miriam's posture, and called, "Please watch my ball, dear." Then he swung.

The ball had struck the bullseye fifteen yards ahead of the men's tee and slightly at an angle. Miriam happened to be standing right there, watching his ball as a good wife should. She had died right there on the seventh tee with only one bruise on her temple.

There were plenty of witnesses. Lester, his hair blown by the gentle breeze, had dropped his club and run to her side. He had, appropriately, called for help. They had, in turn, sent for an ambulance. They had, in turn, called the police. They had, in turn, on the tee and again at the station, questioned Lester and his fellow sportsmen. Everyone had, in turn, agreed upon the tragic accident.

Now it was almost over. Lester pulled from his back pocket a clean handkerchief, recently ironed to perfection by his dutiful wife, and began to wipe his dutifully wet eyes. The linen smelled of Final Touch. Thank God Miriam hadn't thought of poisoning it! That would have been ironic. But it would also have been traceable. She was—had been—smarter than that.

Lester peeked at her angular body, her homely, now-coffined face. The bruise on her temple had been covered cosmetically. She looked peaceful, dear Miriam, utterly content. She would have approved of the blue-flowered dress. The casket was the best he could buy.

As Lester tucked the handkerchief back into his pocket, then picked a bit of lint from the sleeve of his jacket, he wondered what surprise his wife had had in store for him. He smothered a smile. Perhaps she had been planning her move, whatever it was to have been, for the very next hole, the number eight tee.

On the other hand, maybe she had, indeed, been doctoring his food. He hadn't been feeling quite himself lately. Or maybe she had fooled with his rifle. Hunting season was only three months away. Or the brakes on the car? She had been taking a Powerpuff Mechanics class. His benedril capsules?

The balding, bony-fingered minister was standing behind Lester now, patting his shoulder. "Les, would you like to retire to the side room? We'll begin the service whenever you're ready." His smile was sweet.

No side room for Lester, though. He sat brave and straight on the very front row, flanked on one side by his faithful pallbearers, on the other by Miriam's sniveling mother. His eyes were on the Reverend Doctor Tillotson or else on the coffin, its lid now tightly sealed and bedecked with three dozen crimson roses. But his mind was on other, more important matters. What could Miriam have been planning?

Lester when through all the right motions. He bowed his head and following the casket out of the church, supporting his quaking mother-in-law. He followed the hearse down the broad avenue, out to the tree-lined cemetery directly across the road from the golf course. He maintained his rigid composure right through the interment, holding his mother-in-law's clammy left hand, nodding to commiserating spectators.

Then it was over, and Lester had put his mother-in-law into his car. She would, he knew, be a nuisance for a while, but they had never liked each other, and she had her bridge club and her missionary causes. All she could talk about at the moment, however, was the fact that Miriam would miss the Caribbean cruise that she and her mother and her mother's bridge club were to have left on the next day. Lester had convinced his mother-in-law that the bridge club needed her to complete their third table. They would never forgive her if she backed out of the trip. Tearfully, she had agreed. She gave Lester permission to drive her straight back to Bridgeport. She would put into her freezer all the wonderful food her wonderful friends had brought. In spite of overwhelming grief, she would pack tonight and leave in the morning for more pleasant climes.

As he drove back toward home, Lester thought ahead. It would be quiet, peaceful, comfortable, cool. He would check the house slowly and with great care—the food, the medicine, the air conditioner, his pillow. He had plenty of time. And tomorrow he would go for a physical examination, just to be on the safe side. He wanted to enjoy the rest of his life. He would, he decided, skip the golf for the next few days. His buddies would certainly understand. Rain was forecast anyway.

The driveway was steep, for the garage was underground, under the isolated house. The door rose, responding to his electronic instruction. He drove in, easing the Beretta to the front wall. The bumper touched, and he pressed the button again to cause the door to descend. Then, just as the sheet of metal contacted the floor, Lester saw a flash of light overhead. Damn! Something had shorted out. He turned off the lights of the car, but the garage was pitch black, so he pulled them on again. Then he climbed out of the car, heaving a sigh. What a pain! The last time the door had malfunctioned, it had taken two days to get a repairman. This was only a short or a circuit breaker—no big deal. Should be an easy job.

Lester walked to the back of the car. Sure enough, there was a bare wire lying under the door, along the metal track, apparently connected to the fuse box on the wall. How in the hell—?

Then he knew, and cold waves ran through his body. Miriam had booby-trapped the garage, but the car had been undergoing its annual tune-up and so he had not used the garage. Miriam had constantly bragged to anyone and everyone that she was a far better handyman than he. It was true. And had her trick worked three days ago, she would have wept copiously and confessed that this time she had been much, much too careless.

But, Lester frowned, how was this supposed to have killed him? He certainly wasn't dead. He would simply call an electrician later, and in the meantime his worries about her plans were over, and he would simply use her car, parked even now right were she had left it in front of the house, until he could extricate his own.

Lester walked, smiling, to the door that led to the house. He turned the knob. It came off in his hand. He flicked the light switch, but nothing happened. Of course. That, too, had shorted out. In the beams of the headlights, he searched the floor. Then he checked with the flashlight from his glove compartment. The screws for the handle were nowhere to be found. Then he went to the shelf for his tools. He would pry the door open. No! That's right! They were still on the kitchen counter where Miriam said she was working on replacing a pipe under the sink. No tools. God! She had thought of everything.

But ha! there were tools in the trunk of the car. He opened it. The yawning, laughing trunk was bare. There was not so much as a jack. Even the cellular phone, which he had kept in the trunk for emergencies, was missing. Furious, he strode back around and jerked the villainous wire free of the garage door and free of the fuse box. Damn, damn, damn! There had to be a way out. He had been so careful, so respectful—seven years, seven months, the seventh day of the week—.

Lester searched, and Lester scrounged, and finally Lester cried, but his fate had been very neatly sealed.

And that's the way they found him seven days later, starved and dehydrated, long since dead in the burglar-proof garage, sitting disheveled, dirty, and dismally gray on the gray leather seat of his sports car. His body lay slumped over the steering wheel and the horn. The battery of the car was dead. The garage door and the rear bumper of the car were deeply dented, clear evidence of the fact that Lester had tried to ram his way out. Ironic, his buddies and her friends all remarked, that this ideal couple, this model of a pair, should die of two accidents within a few tragic days.

Yes, that's the way they found him, Ron and Bill and Marty said, on a beautiful, sunny, seventh month day that would have been perfect for golf.

*Kelley Jean White*
*Philadelphia, PA*

## Forwarding Addresses

September 1972: my parents borrow Leo's station wagon to move me into the first of six rooms I will live in in Little Hall at Dartmouth over the next four years. A picture of my baby father I've had blown up into a poster fills the back passenger side window. It looks convincingly real.

August 1976: I move onto the fourth floor of Vanderbilt Hall in Boston. My neighbors are convinced that my room is haunted.. They claim everyone who lives there has gone mad. I move out after the first year of medical school.

July 1980: we move to the castle in Philadelphia. Your father figures some guys will happen by and carry our piano up the four flights of stairs. I sit on the porch with your aunties guarding all the furniture on the lawn while he and your uncle go look for movers. At least a dozen people ask the price of my desk.

June 1973: I live in a Forest Service Camp in the White Mountains at Bartlett Experimental Forest. At 3 am every night a tram pulled by four engines passes a few feet from my window. By the end of the first week I sleep right through it. At my going away party I get drunk and stand on the table reciting *How The Grinch Stole Christmas.*

May 1981: I spend Memorial Day weekend painting all eleven rooms of our new twin house across from two abandoned houses on South Saint Bernard Street off white while listening to the three day Beatles marathon on a transistor radio.

April 1956: my parents house comes in prefab pieces on the back of a truck, they put it together in one eight-hour day. I am in the pictures my father labels with each hour, naked except for a diaper, walking through mud.

March 1994 I try to make you love New Hampshire even in mud season by tapping the big maple on the front yard of the old Elsner house in Gilford Village. I have decided to love a house since your father has stopped loving me. I stay up all night boiling sap on the stove. We make two pints of syrup.

February 1978: someone drills a hole through the kitchen door of our apartment in Brookline. Our four classmates in the apartment across the way refuse to talk to the police because it is dinnertime. Another classmate offers to shoot his spear gun through their door.

January 1994: I rent an apartment in the Alden Park Manor over the phone, buy all the cheapest furniture at Ikea, and bring you back to Philadelphia to be near your father.

December 1955: they'd stick a pack of Camels in the back of my diaper and I'd crawl between Auntie Stella and Uncle George's apartment (they were the landlords) and my parents' rooms down the hall. Everyone got together to watch Dragnet.

November 1987: everyday at lunchtime I walk 12 blocks to sit in the backyard
meadow of our new house in Germantown. I think about the ponies and
goats we will keep there, the gardens, the sweet sweet life of our children.
Your brother kicks in my belly.
October 1996: I buy the twin to John's house on Haines Street. I get mad at him
because he smokes a cigar on the front porch on Halloween. All your
friends come over to trick or treat.
September 2003: John sells his house for a fifty percent profit and plans to follow
the trail of Lewis and Clark in his jeep. I am at a loss as to what to do.

–

## *Jewel Delena Quesenberry*
### *Boonevill AR*

## Trapped

A pristine statue of Rebecca stands
in gentle bas-relief
against the gray combination brick
of the planter.
The rank, small jungle of plants
dangles hoydenishly
around her dainty feet.
A tiny black speck, a flea,
crawls confusedly on the immensity
of her hip
her hip has a thrown-out, braced,
sculptured look.
At the opposite side,
on her shoulder, she holds an urn;
her hands vainly reach for the handle
turned 'round to the front.
An embossed, improbable, impossible bowl
sits atop the urn,
and up through this pomposity
a pipe, hollow and threaded
as for a lamp.
Her leg, on that side, is slack, relaxed,
bearing no weight.

Rebecca and I, even at first glance,
are kin; each has a flea upon her hip
and posed in impossible stance,
can not scratch.

*Diana Kwiatkowski Rubin*
*Piscataway NJ*

## Nile Princess

*(for Princess Idut, died in childhood, around 2330 B.C.)*

On this sunset bank,
Waterfowl gather,
Hippos will bathe,
Geese warn overhead.
The horizon radiates.

Tomorrow, child,
Is faraway and asleep,
Underneath alfalfa fields
And shading palms.
A crocodile snaps.

Dreams guard you.
Cunning Osiris watches
Preparing a desert song.
Gods are never cheated.
Soon your heart and soul
Will be poured for measure.

Today, you frolic, unaware,
Among calves and cows
Basking in river valley rays,
A prayer repeating itself.
Immortal spirit, eternity awaits.

* * *

## Diana And Her Companions

*(a painting by Vermeer, 1655-56)*

A captured moment!
Such careful intensity!

Their gazes downward
To her bare white feet
Bathed in translucence
With patience mirrored
In a gleaming gold bowl!

**Carol Dee Meeks**
**Artesia, New Mexico**

## Crushed Rock

When December hardened football fields,
before Christmas, my parent's address
changed. My Dad in shock-six childrenburied
the rock of our family.

Devoured by cancer, we watched her wane away;
two years she laid in dazealert enough
to watch wall clock for nurses
appearance and painkillers.

Her youngest daughter, only six,
and dressed in red;
ushered via the back staircase.
"Beautiful" Mom cried.
She closed both eyes and made
us motherless daughters.

\* \* \*

## Massachusetts Ugly to Visitors

We flew from Albuquerque to Boston with a crowd
of bebop music makers on board. I thought their
noise of un-metered rhyme could not compare
to the cries at the park where the famous green
wall's excitement awaited us. The Yankees were
in town, our favorite team, the reason for our trip.

My spouse wished to take-in the convention,
but our reservations did not match. He from
one party, me the other, we agreed just to get
to come was a treat. He says, "Next year we'll

cruise The USS Constitution in Boston's Harbor."

I said, "Yes, we'll see," doubting we'd be back next
year. I mean, our budget and all. ..from Albuquerque
to Boston every year...once is a lifetime dream.

At Fenway Park the .beboppers showed up. They sat
in the row in front of us. We hardly heard their music,
for Fenway Park's music topped theirs. The Yankees lost.

* * *

*Sharon Ellis*
*Natick MA*

# The Lady in the Story

I am reading "The Yellow Wallpaper" with my seniors.
   More of them complain, "I don't get it," than not.  Mostly the boys, although this is neither unusual nor new.
   I explain, "The protagonist is driven mad with boredom when her husband prescribes rest as a cure.  It's ironic."  I write I-R-O-N-Y on the board and I can hear the pens behind me scribbling it down in their notebooks, like they have swallowed the word without chewing.
   One of the girls asks, "But Miss, why does the lady in the story let her husband keep her cooped up in that room so that she can go crazy?  Why doesn't she just dump him and get out of there?"
   I answer patiently, "Because the story was published in 1892."
   The principal calls me into his office and tells me that I am pushing them too hard.  He sits behind his wood-laminate desk and studies my reaction with his pencil eraser in his mouth.
   I think, *If I don't challenge them, their brains will decay,* but I do not say this out loud.  Instead, I break the principal's stare by looking down at the linoleum peeling away from the floor at the corners like it is trying to escape.  He continues his lecture, adding that feminism is best left to the universities, and that at the rate I'm going none of the girls will ever get into a decent college because I have turned them too political and aggressive.  He says, "The next thing you know you'll be handing out copies of *The Awakening,*" and I make a mental note to cross that off my list of possible novels for next year.
   He concludes that he is going to have to "monitor my syllabus more closely."  Even so, the day after that conversation he asks me casually, while we wait for the drip, drip, drip of the coffee machine in the teacher's lounge to wear itself

out, "So, what are you up to with your seniors these days?"

I tell him, "I am reading 'The Yellow Wallpaper' with my seniors," and he moves his closed mouth from side to side with his eyes narrowed, as if he is trying to taste a flavor that he cannot quite place.

After school I volunteer as a career counselor. One of the girls I counsel has already been accepted to her top three colleges and is trying to narrow down a major. The three course catalogs sit in a neat pile on her desk. She asks me from behind layers and layers of bangs, "What did you study in college?"

I answer, "English, but my thesis was on nineteenth-century women writers."

She wrinkles up her nose and looks surprised. She appears as if she has just spotted a skunk walking into the room.

"It was very interesting," I assure her, "and I earned credit for sitting around reading the books I would have read in my spare time if I had studied something else."

"But what good does that do you now?"

"Well, for example, this year I am reading 'The Yellow Wallpaper' with my seniors."

She snorts out a laugh, "If I wanted to work in the wallpaper department at Home Depot, I wouldn't be going to college, now would I?" She stands up and walks off with her pile of unopened books.

I rush to my car and drive away so that no one I know will see me cry.

I am in the parking lot of the mall. I wander inside and hum a monotone hum in unison with the too-bright lights. There are speakers hidden somewhere in the ceiling pumping out Rolling Stones songs rendered almost unrecognizable by being played on a harp. I stop in one store, but cannot find a single item of clothing bigger than a size two. The next store runs to size twelve, but the saleslady walks next to me as I browse and talks to me like we are friends who are shopping together. When I touch anything she says, "Oh, that suits you," and squeezes my elbow. She is so thin that I rub my stomach every few seconds to make sure it is still there.

I pick up a red dress and the saleslady says, "If you don't mind my saying so, I think that would look perfect on you in saffron."

She holds the saffron dress in front of me and calls out, "Yes, that's it! She looks perfect!" even though there is no other person in the store with us.

"But I like red," I say.

"No," she replies. "Absolutely, the saffron."

Alone in my rented house, I heat a *Lean Cuisine* chicken teriyaki dinner for one in the microwave and finish eating it standing at the kitchen counter while I am still under the pretence of waiting for it to cool down. I am now hungrier than when I started, and I order a pizza.

When I am done with my order, the phone rings in my hand, and I see my brother's name on the caller ID. My brother went to Wall Street instead of college and now his rent is more money than what I earn in two months. He says the same thing he says every week when he calls, "I'm on my cell and I'm on my way to a dinner meeting so I don't have much time. What's new with you?"

I say, "I am reading 'The Yellow Wallpaper' with my seniors."

"I can't make out what you're saying," he yells past the static, "It sounds like you said that you're eating the yellow wallpaper," and I hang up so that he will think his cell phone has lost its signal.

My family envies my brother because he lives a bachelor's life, while they pity me for being the spinster.

The pizza delivery guy says, "Lady, if I had change for a fifty, I wouldn't be driving around with a giant plastic slice of pepperoni pizza on the roof of my car."

"You know," I say, "Preceding a nasty comment with 'Lady' doesn't make it any less rude."

He scratches the too-low back pocket of his jeans with one hand and holds my pizza just out of reach with the other, "Lady, you want the pizza or not?"

I am so hungry and tired that he ends up with a thirty-eight-dollar tip. I am angry and embarrassed so I call after him as he walks down the sidewalk to his car, but the only thing I can think to say is, "I am reading 'The Yellow Wallpaper' with my seniors!"

The words seem to bounce off his raised middle finger.

I dream that night that I am the woman trapped in the room with the terrible yellow wallpaper, but that unlike the lady in the story I stay sane enough so that no one knows anything is wrong. In the morning, I cannot decide which is worse.

While I am getting ready for work, I put on the saffron dress, and suddenly I love it more than I ever could have loved the red one.

I hand out a pop quiz to my seniors. It is the same quiz I give at the end of the first week of every new story or novel we read, the same pop quiz I warned them about two days before. I explain the concept of the quiz in an overly energetic voice meant to make it sound more appealing, "Just to make sure everyone is following along!" Even so, they protest, saying it is not fair and that it sucks.

One boy at the back puts up his hand and says, "You know, my dad says that we shouldn't even be reading this crap. If he writes me a note, do I still have to take the quiz?"

The boy next to him with the gum in his mouth chomps, "Yea. Me too. May I be excused?" Then another boy, and then another.

One of the girls asks, "Don't you think we should read something that might actually be relevant to our lives?"

I take a breath and say quietly, politely, "I am reading 'The Yellow Wallpaper' with my seniors."

*Sandra E. Waldron*
*Olalla, WA*

# Who Was That Guy?

Hunger!

Gripping, stomach-rolling hunger. All Fred could think of was food. He passed his comb through wavy, chestnut hair; splashed after-shave on, tied his white sneakers and wriggled into his maroon OLD NAVY shirt. It was Friday night; available girls would be looking for available guys.

His stomach growled.

A hot tear slid down Jennifer's cheek; she couldn't take much more. Her mother was never home — always slaving away in some greasy café kitchen. And her father? Well, he was eternally drunk. "At least, there's John," she sighed. "Finally, a boyfriend Alice Hicks hasn't stolen from me." She picked up John's photograph and hugged it to her heart, then set it back down. Her cell phone rang.

It was Alice!

She phoned to say John had invited her to dinner, and for Jennifer not to be surprised when he didn't show

Jennifer was too shocked and hurt to reply. She just held the phone away from her face, tearfully listening to Alice's cackling.

She slammed the phone down on her bed. "No more!" she exclaimed, shaking violently.

Her father called from the living room, where he was watching TV. "Jen! Bring me a cold one, will ya?"

She swallowed hard and squinted her eyes, pressing stinging tears away. "Yes, Dad." He needed a beer about as much as she needed Alice.

After she took her dad — who failed to notice she was crying — his beer, she hurried to the bathroom to stare at herself in the mirror. She was pretty. Not beautiful … but pretty. She had her mother's Jewish nose, but it wasn't too big.

So, what's wrong with me? she thought.

The longer she lingered there, the deeper depressed she grew. This was the last straw! She and John had actually spoken of marriage! Eloping, maybe. She'd had no clue … well, maybe a few. He had been very late for their date Wednesday. And he'd forgotten to call her several times lately. She hadn't wanted to see it. It was simply too much.

She desperately needed time to think and decided to take a walk in the park on the beach by the pier. Yes! Right now, it would be so easy to just end it all. The more she thought about it, the more certain she was. Just thinking it made her feel more calm.

She told her father she was taking a walk and left. He barely seemed to notice.

Fred bought a hot dog, but he didn't really want it. He paid the toothless man and went on his way, carrying the unwanted sandwich with him. He spotted a couple of cute blondes with ponytails and bright-pink lipstick. His stomach growled.

Perhaps he could interest one of the girls in a stroll through the park, maybe the pier. Not too many people fishing out there from what he could see.

The pier was long and not well lit on the end. A good place to take a girl ... and eat. He looked at his uninteresting hot dog and moved towards the girls. He stopped. Two guys approached. They seemed to know the girls. No good. He'd be better off finding a lone girl. Make things more ... simple.

It was dark when Jennifer reached the park. A cool wind had blown in, bringing with it a misty, icy rain, but it wasn't enough to discourage the young people in the park. She stepped up to the pier, glad to see it was almost deserted. One black man was fishing about midway across. She passed him, listening to old boards squeak under her feet, thinking someone should replace them before an accident happened. How convenient it would be if she were the one to fall through. She chuckled sardonically at the notion.

Fred took several bites of his hot dog, but he didn't swallow. When no one was looking, he spit the chewed wad into a bush. He continued on along the joggers' path and passed an elderly couple, walking arm in arm. He heard the old woman say, "Such a nice looking young man ... Don't you think, Harry?"

Fred sniggered to himself.

That's what everyone thought. His stomach reminded him of his increasing need for nourishment. He had to get something decent to eat soon. His eyes lit up when he noticed the redhead walking by herself onto the pier. Convenient. He tossed his hot dog in the gently rippling waves and advanced quickly to the pier.

The black man who'd been fishing was leaving. He nodded to Fred. Fred nodded back.

The water seemed so peaceful to Jennifer. It could wash away all her pain and suffering. It would be so easy she jerked back with a start when the tall young man came up behind her. "Nice evening," he said, knowing it was beginning to rain.

"It is?" She was disappointed. She really wanted to be alone. Her gaze turned back out to the gray water, watching it slap against the support poles of the pier.

"You ... by yourself?" he asked cautiously.

She studied his darkly handsome face. His yellow eyes seemed to glow. There was something about him that frightened her. She really shouldn't admit she was alone. This man, though very handsome and charming, was a stranger. But then, why was she worrying? "Yes," she confessed.

He salivated.

"What's a nice girl like you doing out here?" he asked lightly.

"I want to be alone. That's why I'm here." She hoped he'd take the hint.

She was depressed about something. That made things even better. "I'm a good listener. Want to talk about it?"

"No! Just go away!"

Her harshness failed to move him. "Not thinking of ending it all, are you?"

Her brow furrowed. "How'd you know?"

"Oh ... I can tell."

She found his calmness infuriating. "Get out of here!"

He blew at a wisp of hair that had fallen in his eyes, all the while, holding her gaze. "If you really want to kill yourself, perhaps I can be of some assistance?"

"What? What kind of nut are you?"

"Not anymore nuts than you. You admitted you wanted to end it all."

"No! I didn't."

"Yes you did," he insisted.

"Will you please go away? Leave me alone?"

"Are you going to kill yourself?"

"I ... I really don't know."

"If you're not sure, then you probably won't."

"Well, it's my business, if I want to kill myself, isn't it?"

His eyes smiled. "Tell you what. I'll walk a little ways down the pier. I'll wait. If you find you don't have the guts to do it, call me. Okay?"

"You're not serious ... are you?"

He grinned unnervingly. "Very."

He means it! God! He really means it.

Suddenly, she wasn't so sure she wanted to die. "Please! Just go away." She turned away from his stare and looked out at the water again. She heard him walk off, and she relaxed a little. But he didn't go very far. She realized how very quiet everything was, the only sound being that of the slapping waves. She glanced back in the direction of the park. Deserted. Rain drummed the ground. Everyone had gone home or someplace out of the wet. Her hands trembled.

"Made your decision yet?" he called to her.

She didn't want to answer. What was she going to do? She was all alone on this pier with a stranger —some kind of weirdo who seemed all too willing to help her die.

Fred grew impatient. Silly female, he thought. She was ready to kill herself until I came along. Now, she's not so sure. Figures. I can tell. She's nervous. And, I'm hungry!

A lone gull from overhead called out, searching for others of his kind. Jennifer wished she were a gull and could just fly away.

"Have you decided?" Fred asked impatiently.

"Yes!" she blurted. "I have changed my mind. I don't want to die!"

"Just like a woman!" he snorted, then started towards her.

She backed away and found herself against the rail. He was in front of her, staring at her with those fiery, yellow eyes. "I don't want to die. It was silly of me to think I wanted to. I don't need your help. I just want to go home."

"But what about my dinner? I'm hungry."

"Huh? Hungry? What's that got to do with me?'

He smiled hugely, revealing two, very long incisors.

She gulped this can't be real! She tried inching her way along the railing, but he grabbed her.

"It's what you wanted. You know, this could go on and on ... you're changing your mind. Let's make it simple and get it over with."

"No! No! I won't! Let me go!" She managed to slip from his grip and started running ... running and screaming.

There was hallow thudding as their feet flew over the old planks. The rain came down hard and beat in their faces.

Jennifer called out for help, but everyone was gone. She ran and ran, knowing her life depended on it. The more she ran, the more she knew she wanted to live. There was her poor mother. She hadn't been thinking of her at all. She had been selfish, really selfish, thinking she wanted to end it all.

Fred almost caught up with her, then slipped on a loose board. He regained his footing and took after her again. She was off the pier now, and a pickup all but flew into the park. The truck slowed down.

Jennifer stopped in her tracks. She recognized the truck immediately. It was John's! He and Alice Hicks got out. They were arguing about something. Jennifer's name was mentioned. They were fighting over her. "I shouldn't have stood Jennifer up to go out with you," he said.

"You're not going back to that skinny worm, are you?"

"Yes! If she'll have me."

"Oh ... oh no you won't! I'll tell her everything!"

"You would, too, wouldn't you? Go ahead. I'm still gonna try. I can only blame myself, if she won't have me. It's all my fault for ever looking at you."

Fred caught up with Jennifer. There was nothing he could do but stand there and listen with her. "You know those two?"

"Yeah. That's my ex-boyfriend, John. And that ... female is Alice Hicks."

"Cozy," he snorted. Surely his stomach would cave in from starvation He had to eat!

Suddenly, Alice noticed the drenched and dripping Jennifer standing at the end of the pier, watching them. "How much did you hear? You little " then she laid eyes on Fred. She gasped, "What a hunk!"

John had a sudden sinking feeling in his stomach. It was too late; Jennifer had herself a new boyfriend. It was what he deserved. What could he expect other than what was his due.

Already, Alice approached Fred and Jennifer, forgetting John. "Hi! Jennifer. How's 'bout introducing me to your new boyfriend?" She took Fred in from head to foot with greedy eyes. This one she had to have! No way, was Jennifer good enough for this guy.

Jennifer's eyes darted back from Fred to Alice and from Alice to Fred. "Oh ... Alice, I don't think you want "

"Hello! Handsome!" she said, ignoring Jennifer. "Where's she been hiding you?"

Fred smiled secretively to Jennifer.

She stared at him speechless for a moment, then slowly began to return his smile.

"I really don't think you can handle this one, Alice."

Alice scoffed. "There ain't no man I can't handle."

"But this one's ... special."

Alice rolled her eyes. "You've always been such a nerd, Jennifer. Of course, I can see he's special. That's why I'm gonna have him instead of you!"

"Really ... "

Alice paid her no heed. Fred took her by the arm and led her away down the pier.

"Nice knowing you, Fred, " Jennifer called.

Fred grinned like a Cheshire over his shoulder and waved.

John was puzzled. "Who in heck was that guy?"

"Aw … just a friend."

"Is that all … really? I was worried he was your new boyfriend."

"It would serve you right, but he's not."

"Wow! You have no idea what a relief it is to hear you say that." He opened his truck door and helped her in.

Just as they pulled away, a chilling scream cut through the night air. John jerked his head around.

"Did you hear that?"

"Hear what?" she said innocently, and quickly rolled her window up. "The rain's getting harder and the wind's picking up."

"I could have sworn I heard a woman scream."

"I didn't hear a thing, John. Must be the wind whistling across the pier," she lied. She had heard it clearly.

He listened intently for a moment. The only sound was that of drumming rain. "Yeah … guess you're right…. This has been one strange night."

"You can say that again," she said, and she smiled a very satisfied smile.

*Darrel Roberto Mickel*
*New York, NY*

### 'Darklights'

I can see her perfumed shadow
on moonbeams that glow
her face seeming
to replace all the stars
that ever were. . .
and I see through
darkness and light's
cascading sorrow
so . . . the time for remembering shadows
that have thrilled me illuminate once more

**Michael Fitzgerald**
**Winchester, VA**

## The Last Half-Acre

The last lot, the last half-acre
in my Shenandoah town has been
bought,

The county around us had one or two
planners when I was growing up
now they have thirteen.

Just over the Blue Ridge lies
the fastest growing county
in the entire United States.

The Shenandoah National Park
got one of the worst ratings for air quality
truckers on I-8l   down the lungs of the Valley.

Back in the 1930s you used to be
able to go up on the top of the Blue Ridge
and see the Washington Monument..

No way today.  Even on the clearest day,
an eerie, gray haze rises above
the city of Washington
as the engines grind on.

**Barbara D. Holender**
**Snyder NY**

## In Longwood Gardens

*Let's go,* you said, charging down the path
through blurs of begonias massed in reds,
zinnias, delphinium and dahlias.
You never stopped for breath.

*Come on,* you said, in the Italian water garden,
its variant fountain pools sculptured in perspective
to assume the same dimensions from the viewing bridge
we sped across.

We did the Conservatory in fifteen minutes,
including the water lilies' giant platter pads
capable of bearing one hundred and fifty
well-distributed pounds.

In the Arboretum I noted forms
of cypress, juniper and yew
(*While the world goes by,* you said)
and stopped to read the name
of a smooth-boled tree hung high with pods.
*It's* a *tree,* you cried, a *tree is* a *tree.*

Flying from your dirty city to my dirty city
little faster than we had flown through the gardens,
I swung by my prehensile mind
slowly from the bald cypress knees
to the pale pods of the princess tree.


\* \* \*


## A Birthday

My feet are 77.
They look it
puffing at the ankles
collecting themselves
to shoot the dark veins
up the knotty trunks.
I travel light,
hope they'll hold me.

But if I must go piecemeal
I'd rather go from below
like Socrates
conversant to the end

than grope the long way down
having thrown
the master switch.


\* \* \*

## Suddenly Everyone's Dying

It's like wandering through a night forest
haunted by Blakeian shades,
hearing a "thunk" -uh-oh,
now who's down?
hardly daring to breathe
the mushroom fog, brushing
the webs from arms, face,
ducking the swish of the sword
overhead, not my turn,

naming the fallen
sleep, sleep so close,
so missed, so dear
all night so sad dreaming

and at dawn so glad
so glad just to wake.

*A. M. Donovan*
*Kuna, ID*

## Garbage

Old dreams discarded
By the roadside
Amongst old fast food wrappers
Beer bottles, and dead animals
Dreams
Broken by the world
A world in which
They couldn't survive
Or abandoned, like a puppy
To ridicule and shame
Outgrown, outmoded, thrown away
Some will come back, briefly
Into vogue
Like patriotism, and faith
Or lets whisper God
Then we dig, frantically
Through the detritus of our lives
Trying to find
The newly realized treasure

*Richard Owen*
*Orrville OH*

# Maglop

The prisoner paced incessantly in his eight by ten cell silently plotting his next escape attempt, deep in the dark fortress of the old penitentiary in solitary confinement. He had little access to the outside world, or even the inside, as he had become a notoriously clever escape artist who not only brilliantly schemed and dreamed of escape, but also had quite often successfully scaled or burrowed his way out —only to be eventually recaptured.

He wickedly laughed, and paused in his persistent pacing to recall how he had contemptuously and brazenly escaped in the past. It was as if he was the star in "Hogan's Heroes," and the guards like Klink and Schultz, bunglingly inept in their feeble attempts to quash his effortlessly amusing antics in the stalag. At first his abilities were considered naughty, or impiously disconcerting, but as time went on and his infamously ingenious natural talent as a villainous Houdini became more ominous, he became the bane of the prison.

The key to his success, the prisoner knew, was not only his persistent nature, but also his uncanny presence to use any device imaginable to win his freedom. He possessed a charming wit, and when confronted with adversity he used his intelligence to reason, and even tempt others to abet him with escape.

What pleased him most were the escapes when he was not even detected until his flagitious nature made others aware that he was, once again, running amok. Gleefully gloating, knowing that his next plan would surely work, the prisoner patiently awaited his move. For this was not only the greatest chess match of all time to him, it was all he lived for.

Time was his greatest ally, for time was nothing of consequence to him. He had the rest of his life to make the next move, as he was serving a life sentence.

\*

The guard assigned to watch over the infamous prisoner stared at him on a monitor in the nerve center of the old prison, far from the dank dungeon where the rebellious escape artist was now confined. Even though safe in the nexus of the upper tier of the guard office, the guard shivered involuntarily as a cold chill tingled down his spine staring at the malevolent grin of the prisoner.

The guard, named Jacob after his father who was the previous warden of the prison, recalled the first time he had laid eyes upon Prisoner 17925. His father had given young Jacob a tour of the prison when he was eight. He had been awestruck by the starkness of the old stone-hewn penitentiary, and scared of being in the prison even though escorted by his large, strong father who smilingly greeted the prison trustees and others who milled about the vast prison yard. That was when young Jacob first noticed a rather tall, good-looking man in standard blue prison garb watching him as he crossed the yard with his father. His ice-blue eyes tracked young Jacob, and Jacob felt the hairs on the back of his neck stand on end.

His father, noticing his discomfort, asked him, "What's wrong, Jacob?"

Jacob barely was able to stutter, "W-w-ho's that man watching me, Dad?"

His father's deep smile creases disappeared as he focused on the staring prisoner. "That, Jacob, is a very bad man. His name is Maglop."

Maglop casually strode across the compound stopping a few yards short of them, smiled widely and showed his perfect white teeth. Waving, he greeted them, "Hello, Warden, that's a fine looking young man you have with you. He must be your son, the family resemblance is there!"

Young Jacob smiled back at Maglop. But his father rather sternly replied, "Move along Maglop, get back to your area."

Maglop continued smiling and nodding agreement replied, "Why of course, Warden, just admiring your fine son." Maglop backed slowly away and continued to smile at young Jacob, and as Jacob watched, Maglop quickly winked at him, turned and walked back towards the other prisoners.

Little Jacob turned his head up to see his father frowning as he remarked, "Dad, he seems like a nice man."

His father looked down and quietly answered, "Yes, son, he does. But as you will find out in life, things aren't always what they seem."

*

Maglop peered at the security camera, his senses so finely tuned that he could actually feel Jacob monitoring him. The longer he stared into the tiny camera lens, the greater he could feel and almost taste Jacob's fear. He felt that he could clairvoyantly make out his thoughts as they both stared at each other, transfixed with this fusion of mind.

Maglop's power had grown through his years of confinement. He had been able to muster a great deal of time, thought, and energy into his paranormal ability of reaching out with his thoughts and finding a donor-host that he could psychically touch. This had made him strong in finding weaknesses of others, or the prison defenses, which enabled him to find daring, devious, and diabolical ways of escaping.

From the first time he had met young Jacob, he sensed a psychic link between them. He knew, even then, that destiny would someday take young Jacob to follow in the footsteps of his father to work in the prison.

Feeding on the fear he felt, he grew stronger. His senses became more acute, and with a detached part of his peripheral senses he saw an approaching storm. Darkness grew in the moonless night, and large drops of cold rain began pounding the ancient walls of the gothic prison. High above lightning struck, only to be smothered in the ebony folds of the blackened clouds. The wicked wind howled relentlessly upon the guard towers, and even the spotlights looked dimmed in the murky maelstrom. The black-cloaked storm soon reached frenzied chaos, and although deep underground in his solitary cell shut off from all light and sound, Maglop heard the thunder-rolls and saw the lightning strike above in the turbulent air.

He smiled.

Reaching through the tons of mortar and stone with his prescient spirit, Maglop touched the ionized storm with his mind. Reaching further into the blackened night, he felt a bolt of lightning's birth and guided its head through the dark womb-tomb to strike the main prison generator.

A brilliant clap of raw power blew the generator apart, and instantly blanketed the prison in black.

\*

Jacob responded by instinct. With his bank of monitors dead and only a dim glow of the emergency lights bathing the control room, he quickly flicked the back-up generator on and checked the current read-outs to the electrified barbed-wire fences surrounding the maximum-security prison.

Next, he scanned the color-coded panel for all lock-downs then reset the security monitors. That was the only problem. Perhaps it was a quirk, but some of the monitors were emanating scrambled pictures or just static. The only logical explanation was that the bolt of lightning had fried some circuitry. He finished by checking the communications, and they all seemed to be in order, so he called his electrical maintenance man to get to work on the malfunctioning monitors.

This extraordinary situation had never occurred before, in Jacob's memory, but he had responded efficiently to the emergency and was quite proud that nothing disastrous had occurred.

Control was something Jacob took great pride in. Whenever he had been put under duress he had always responded with remarkable stoicism. The storm reminded him of the last great storm the prison had endured, the night he came close to losing his mind; the greatest trial he had ever faced in his life. The night he had found his father hanging from an oak beam over his desk.

Jacob had not been working as a guard at the prison for very long when he noticed his father becoming increasingly despondent and withdrawn. Still, it had been a great shock to find his father slowly swinging with a noose around his neck after jumping off from his desk.

He realized that for that reason he was probably going to have to wait a long time to advance in position at the prison. The new warden, and even the assistant warden, kept a jaundiced eye upon him; *did they think he was capable of following his father's path of self-destruction?*

That was why he was putting more and more time working at the prison. He had something to prove, not only to others, but also to himself. That was why he was working extra shifts and ignoring his family responsibilities.

Deep in thought, Jacob was just recalling how he had felt strangely drained while staring at his nefarious prisoner, Maglop, when the power surge had startled him out of his reverie. Glancing quickly at Maglop's monitor, it was emitting nothing but static. Thinking he should call to double-check on his status with the Isolation Officer, Jacob felt a cold chill run up his spine. *What is it?* he mused, and almost jumped out of his skin hearing a deep chuckle behind him.

Wheeling, he faced the pernicious smile of Maglop.

\*

Swallowing a stifled curse, Jacob froze in shock. Maglop was five feet behind him, alone in the control room with him. Maglop was standing relaxed and smiling, but his icy eyes were ablaze with scorn, melting all resistance Jacob had.

"H-h-ow did you get in here," Jacob stammered. He knew that Maglop would have had to pass several checkpoints and locked doors to get there.

Maglop smiled, "Jacob, it was you who let me out."

Jacob flared, in anger and fear, "Right, *I* let *you* out!"

Maglop quietly continued to madly grin and pointed toward the security panel, "Look at it, Jacob."

Jacob trembled as he noticed the toggle switches to Maglop's cell, and all access doors leading to him were turned off. He cringed weakly, "I d-d-don't understand…"

"You have been too blind to see, Jacob. You decided to let me out. I think we both have known for some time that you wanted to."

Violently shaking his head, Jacob denied Maglop, "No way, it is my job to make sure that you *don't* escape."

Shaking his head in return, and condescendingly smirking, Maglop simply stated, "Think, Jacob, you have been calling me for some time now."

Trembling with fear, Jacob gasped, *"Who are you?"*

Maglop stepped close to Jacob and replied in his undisguised, deep, malignant, and resonant voice, *"We are legion!"*

A scream of terror erupted and died in Jacob's frozen throat.

"Do not deny me, Jacob. It is written that no man can serve two masters. I have been awaiting your call since that time I first met you as a little boy, not even knowing your destiny."

Stunned, too frightened to even attempt speech, Jacob stared openly at the prisoner.

"You see, Jacob, I have always been with you, since your age of accountability. I have known your every desire, need, and thought. You are a chosen spirit, and we have known each other for millennia."

Jacob's puzzled face drew a heavy sigh from the execrable spirit facing him. "That's right, Jacob, you don't have a full recollection of your immortal existence. But I do."

Motioning to a chair, Maglop coaxed Jacob to sit. Jacob sunk heavily into the seat. His knees felt weak; he couldn't have stood for another minute. Maglop pulled up another chair and facing Jacob continued his explanation.

"I have no reason to lie to you, now. In the beginning we were close friends, Jacob. We were bright intelligences perfect in form, and eternal in being. Then, a council was held to vote on how we could best be tested to further our eternal progression. We all decided the best plan was for us to gain mortal bodies, to be subjected to disease, death, and most importantly, have a veil placed over our post-mortal memories, so that we could not recall our former estate and being. That way we could best be tested, not knowing who we were."

A glimmer of interest and understanding passed over Jacob's face as Maglop continued, "There were two camps divided on how this feat was to be accomplished. One, to have free agency, and let each individual spirit make their own choices while in mortal life, and the other, to be forced to obey, making sure that all spirits would successfully pass the test."

"You, Jacob, chose the former. I followed the Son of Morning's plan, assuring that all would be saved. A great contention ensued, a battle fought, and my side lost. You and your side got your wish, and obtained mortal bodies."

Maglop glared evilly at Jacob, "Yes, Jacob, I was cast from our heavenly home to never experience what you have...a body. I am a spirit who was assigned to be your host while you are here. Your tempter, to entrap you in whatever way I can to ensnare your soul."

Jacob trembling heavily, found his voice. "But I don't choose you...I choose God!"

Enraged at the sound of the Almighty Maker's name, Maglop furiously spat, *"NO,* you have chosen *ME!* When you weakened yourself with drugs and alcohol; when you chose to hide from your family responsibility with your work; when you allowed me to allure and invite you to perform unseemly acts, you were choosing me, Jacob!"

Jacob, scared, as blood drained from his face, shivered in remembrance of his sins. "But..."

Maglop derisively hooted, "You don't need to make excuses to *me* Jacob, remember, I know you and all of your weaknesses!"

Large tears welled in the eyes of Jacob.

Maglop solicitously sneered, "Don't feel bad Jacob, it happens to the best, and we, my friend, have only just begun."

Maglop sprang from his seat into the shocked body of Jacob.

Klaxons wailed throughout the compound.

The prisoner had escaped again.

*

Jacob felt a cold spirit envelope him, as Maglop possessed his body with the power of his strong, satanic force of blackness. He sat stunned, unable to stand or even speak. He looked out upon the world around him with a different set of eyes. Now he understood why he had been fascinated with Maglop, why he had felt strangely drawn to him. Sadness began to saturate his soul, but before he could begin to feel sorry for himself and his predicament, Maglop pushed his conscious thoughts aside, like an unwanted toy, and took over every thought.

Gleefully triumphant, Maglop insinuated, "Now, Jacob, that wasn't so bad was it?"

Jacob had little time to muse that it only took seconds of weakness in a lifetime to allow this beast possession of his body. Without any time to rue, Maglop began taking action.

"Cheer up, Jacob," Maglop purred, "you will be doing far greater things than you ever have in your life of tedious boredom, and you will be meeting much more interesting people than you ever have...starting tonight!"

Search parties were formed after a count revealed that the prisoner Maglop was missing. Maglop chuckled, with joy, in the mind of Jacob, as Jacob went through the motions of organizing the search, for a prisoner who had the perfect hideout- the guard supervisor's body.

The warden had to be called in, as protocol demanded, and Jacob made the call.

"Warden Hasting," Jacob told the sleepy, grouchy voice, "this is Jacob. I'm afraid I have some bad news."

A quizzical voice snapped, "What is it?"

Jacob paused before answering with an audible gulp, "Maglop has escaped again, sir."

A longer pause met Jacob's ear. A slightly bemused warden finally responded, "Oh he has, has he? Well, I'll be right in then."

The line went dead in Jacob's ear, and as he dropped the phone into it's cradle, Maglop hysterically laughed in Jacob's confused mind. "You have nothing to worry about, Jacob, everything is falling into place."

Shaving his sculptured face in the bathroom mirror, the warden tried not to grin too hard. He didn't want to cut his handsome mug.

\*

Warden Hasting impatiently awaited the arrival of Jacob in his office, only an hour after his call. He ruefully eyed the large oak beam overhead, where Jacob's father had been found swinging such a short time ago.

Jacob was ushered into the warden's office by the sleepy-eyed secretary, who had been called into work two hours earlier than normal to handle all the phone calls generated by the breakout.

"Jacob," smiled the suddenly happy warden, "sit; make yourself at home."'

As Jacob sat, his eyes flared a deep scarlet. A resonant bass voice growled, "No need for cheap charm, warden, it is me...Maglop!"

The warden's eyes glowed red, and the false smile slide from his face as Maglop continued with a deep-throated chuckle, "Jacob, meet Belial."

Jacob, cornered into a small part of his mind, shivered with the sudden realization that he was not the only one possessed.

Belial/Hastings evilly sneered at Maglop/Jacob and eyeing the overhead oak beam, snarled, "Your father wasn't as reasonable as you, Jacob."

It dawned on Jacob that his father had not committed suicide, as he had been led to believe. Belial and Maglop impishly giggled at the involuntary spasm of Jacob. Belial glowered, "Yes, Jacob, your father met his end because he refused to cooperate. Never forget that you can end up in the same place," he laughed, mockingly pulling his tie up from his neck as he eyed the beam.

"We have nothing to fear from this one," laughed Maglop, "He understands his place, and soon will understand his place in history!"

After the warden had called off the search, he made a few placating phone calls to assure authorities that the missing prisoner would soon be apprehended.

"Haven't we always found him?

"He can never make it out of the swamp!"

Jacob and Hastings then left the prison in a state-issued Jeep.

The prison, located in the middle of the Everglades, housed Florida's most notorious prisoners, and it served to keep prisoners away from public view, and conversely, it kept the public away from the prison.

A short distance from the prison, Hastings turned off the only road leading away from the penitentiary onto a small, seldom-used trail that led into a mangrove swamp. They parked near a camouflaged airboat, and they quickly disembarked and tore the tarp from the boat and jumped in. Minutes later, after negotiating across the desolate swamp, they turned into an inlet that took them to a secluded cabin on small island.

A lazy-looking, curious gator eyed Jacob tie off the boat as Hastings covered the airboat with the camo tarp, then they headed into the small sun-bleached wood cabin.

Hastings opened a hidden safe, pulled out some charts and other papers, and laid them on the rustic table in the middle of the one-room cabin. Grinning hugely, Jacob sat down as Maglop growled, "Now, it all begins."

*

Jacob recoiled at the musty, decayed odor of the old cabin, as beads of sweat formed all over him in the humid, oppressive heat.

"You look a little confused, Jacob," Hastings/Belial grinned, "but don't worry, you will soon find out what is going on."

After unrolling the charts, Hastings spread them out on the moldy, old desk. Maglop peered at the papers, and smilingly asked, "Everything going according to plan then?"

Belial returned the evil smile and replied, "Everything is proceeding smoothly. The men are finishing with their training soon; success will be ours!"

Belial's eyes turned brilliantly red as he roared triumphantly, "Jacob, Jacob, since time immemorial it has been our mission to usurp, confuse, frighten, and do anything we can to destroy the destiny of man, along with his dreams and beliefs in goodness and eternal happiness. From the beginning of time, from Cain to Khomeini, we have worked for the Prince of Darkness to fulfill his plans."

Belial stood, and pacing around the table stressed his spiel. "We choose those who we know will help us with our cause. History is replete with those great ones who have submitted to our will to subvert the plans of the Creator. You may recall even the great King Saul was host to us, and in his jealous rage attempted time after time to destroy his chosen successor, David."

Maglop smiled and agreed with Belial. "War is our friend, the greatest destroyer of peace, love, and harmony. For with death and destruction man's spirit is turned, and will serve our Master. At this moment, the greatest of our warriors is preparing for the beginning of the end of all time."

Belial shook his head in affirmation, "Yes, Jacob, you are host to one of our Master's greatest warriors, in might and intelligence. It is he who has conceived this great plan to bring about the culmination of His Great Destiny!"

Sneering, Maglop explained, "Belial, as you know, I am just adapting a plan already devised in the most innocuous way. Jacob, have you read the works of the popular novelist, Tom Clancy?"

*

Fifty aeronautical miles away, Atta/Bezel maneuvered his Cessna trainer into a landing on the remote landing strip on the edge of the Everglades. He glared hatefully at his female instructor in the co-pilot seat as she praised him for the perfect landing.

*

Jacob's blood ran cold; he no longer sweated in the hot ride back to the prison. His orders were to act normal and return home to his family. He thought he could no longer be "normal" again. At home, his three young children ran excitedly towards him as he entered the front door. But a glance at his eyes made them back away from him and run to get Mom instead.

Jenna knew instantly that something was wrong with Jacob. She had seen that look of despair before, and the redness of his eyes bespoke his countless episodes with drugs and alcohol. She turned tearfully away without even greeting him and went back to her housework.

*Sometimes I wonder what I ever saw in him!* She cried in her heart as she fled his presence, just as her little ones had.

Jacob sadly covered his well-worn path to the study, his refuge, and the half-bottle of rum hidden in the closet.

*

Belial sat with his feet propped up on his desk. Staring up at the oak beam overhead, he grinned, "Yes, old Jacob, it won't be long now. Victory is ours!"

*

Halfway around the world, meditating on his barren floor at the beginning of a new day, the prone supplicant had his ear whispered into by the Old Serpent, "Yes, praise your Master. Soon your devils will all be crying in the darkness of their souls!"

*

Jacob's reverie was broken by a small voice. "Daddy, you look so tired…why aren't you in bed?" Jacob turned his troubled head to see his little one, Christina, crawl up into his lap. Although his heart melted to see the pure innocence of his three-year-old youngest, his body stiffened as Maglop, once again, took control over him. Before he could respond to his little angel, Christina looked up into his eyes and softly chided him, "Daddy, you don't look well. We are all worried about you."

He managed to rasp, "You're right, little one, I think it's time for both of us to get some sleep."

Jacob clumsily carried his little girl to her bed, and turning to leave heard her plaintiff request, "Daddy, aren't you going to give me a goodnight kiss?"

He slowly leaned over to kiss her little lips, but felt her shiver upon touching them. "B-r-r-r, Daddy, your lips are so cold!"

Robot-like he turned quietly away, but felt a small tear run from the corner of one eye as he made an exit from her room.

*

The next few days were a blur as Jacob went through the motions at work, meeting often with Hastings plotting their every move. It wasn't long before another road trip north, to Orlando, took them to a meeting at a Day's Inn to meet a group of sullen men.

Jacob was introduced to several other men, who had all arrived separately to meet them. They were all Mid-Eastern, and as somber as Hastings and Jacob. Hastings took control of the meeting, and smiling coldly at them, told the group that the time was near. They had all been booked on various flights to their destinations. Hastings reminded each of them how easy it was going to be. How they were soon to wreck havoc upon the Great Nation who presumed to be the world dictator. He reminded them of Clancy's book, *Debt of Honor*, and how easy it was going to be to bring the tyrants of injustice to their knees.

A chorus of cheers broke out, and they departed to their destinations.

\*

Jacob quietly told his family goodbye, that he had business to attend to out-of-town, and turned to leave. Little Christina ran to him and hugged his legs from behind. "Don't forget, I love you Daddy!"

Hastings and Jacob set quietly beside each other on their flight to Boston. They were on the red-eye early morning commuter flight with a connection to Los Angeles later in the morning. Before dawn they were at Logan drinking a cup of coffee together before heading for the United terminal. Several times they looked up to secretly eye other men who were heading to their own flights.

At the United terminal they gave their tickets to the clerk and announced they had no baggage, just a carry-on each, and leisurely strolled to their gate. In line for Flight 93, they noticed two comrades who had been with them, days earlier, in Orlando. As they made their way to their seats in the mid-rear section, Hastings grinned malevolently at Jacob and coldly stated, "It is time!"

\*

Jet engines screamed as they lunged down the runway and roared into the early morning air over the Atlantic, before turning slowly west and banking over the bustling city of Boston.

Sweat trickled down Jacob's forehead as he eyed the back of Hastings' head directly in front of him. Nervously, he pretended to read a flight magazine from the seat pocket in front of him, but he noticed he was gripping the magazine so tightly that his knuckles were turning white.

Minutes agonizingly slowed into hours as he forced himself to relax, and not think about time. From behind him a familiar face passed forward down the aisle. The swarthy man smirked at him, just as Hastings, wearing an earplug from a radio, turned to Jacob and whispered, "Success!"

A scream interrupted the quiet flight, and just as quickly stopped. Confusion and commotion broke out in front of them. A stewardess announced, with great tension, "Please remain calm."

Jacob/Maglop leaned forward and whispered into Hastings ear, "We've done it! We are in control!"

A small group of men were talking tersely in front of them. Jacob caught a little of the conversation. "Terrorists!"

A small, dark-haired man strode towards them with a blooded sheetrock knife in front of him. "Silence...or *you* will die next!"

The jet veered sharply to the left; they were turning toward their target.

Concerned, whispered voices, rising in agitation, reached Jacob. Hastings/Belial turned to Jacob and cursed, "They are going to try something...get ready!"

Maglop fumed. From all accounts success had already taken place. The Trade Center was ablaze and the Pentagon had been taken out. They were destined to kamikaze the White House or the Capitol, like the Clancy villain had done in his JAL jet. He fumbled for his knife in his attaché case under his seat.

A group of passengers had risen in front of them with a shout, and were starting to charge toward the cabin. Hastings/Belial already had his knife out and was rising, raising his arm to drive the point into the rebel in front of him.

Jacob/Maglop rose behind him, and something snapped in Jacob's mind. Before Maglop could react, Jacob grabbed the hair of Hastings with his left hand and drew his knife through his soft neck.

Maglop raged inside of Jacob, but as hard as Maglop pushed he could not get Jacob to get up from his seat to stop the rioting and take-over of the aircraft.

Furious, Maglop began to psychically hammer Jacob's brain with all of his strength.

The sickening g-force of the jet pushed Jacob's body deeper into his seat. Blood oozed from his ears as the engines screamed its spiral death-throe to the ground.

Jacob's last thought was of his family. He heard little Christina in his mind, "Daddy, I love you!"

Flight 93 plunged into the ground and all life ceased aboard in the massive explosion.

*

Jacob floated through the air, he felt so light. A marvelous light beckoned to him, and a pure whiteness filled his soul. He was facing his father, who was smiling at him. "You have done well, my son. You have fulfilled your mission; I am *so* proud of you!"

*

A blackened spirit wafted and hiked the desolate Pennsylvania countryside. Cursing, in hatred and malignant madness, he laughed...

The prisoner had escaped again.

*Manuel Garcia-Barrio*
*Philadelphia, PA*

# Saint Wayne

The taped-up plastic rotary phone on the dresser rang. Shamiq Thompson put down the spiral notebook full of his rap lyrics, jumped off the lower bunk, then decided to let the answering machine get it. Shamiq shared the room with his older brother Wayne whenever Wayne wasn't out of town in Virginia or the Carolinas, unloading keys or half keys on consignment from Little Pacino or Tray Ball, which must be where he was en route to now, since Wayne's jet-black Acura legend coupe wasn't parked out on Eleventh. Shamiq wished Wayne would let him come along; anything to get away from Richard Allen Housing Projects, home to crackheads by the flock and rats the size of cats. Shamiq's mother was away, working the early shift at Hahnemann Memorial. She'd get off around ten and catch the Market Street Subway to the KFC in the subway concourse under City Hall for the opening shift there. And Shamiq would rehearse for the twice-yearly talent show at William Pen High School. If he made the grade there, Shamiq's mother said whenever he saw her, he might get into Central as a sophomore, and graduate into U of Penn after his senior year.

The answering machine cut in on the fourth ring.

"Yo, this Wayne 'Super Hood' Thompson. I'm either away on business or in here strippin' some fashion model, word is bond. Just leave a name and number and I'll get up with you whenever I got my hands free. Peace."

Shamiq picked up his book of rap lyrics and stood in front of the mirror, glancing at the framed picture of Wayne that hung above his bunk where the cross grandma gave him for his eleventh birthday used to hang. Big bro sat on the hood of the Acura, black forty-five automatic standing out against the gray boxers peeking over the waist of his low-slung black jeans, shirt off, muscles impossibly large, BLACK ESCOBAR tattoed on his chest and stenciled across his windshield.

Shamiq saluted Big Bro's image as the machine beeped.

"Wayne, it's detective Claiborne from the thirty-fifth. I hear you failed to show up at Judge Macmillan's courtroom this morning. I'm not going to be able to bail you out of too many more… well, you know. Give me a call; you know my pager number."

Shamiq wondered why the cops were calling his big brother. Wayne hated cops. He, Tray Ball and Little Pacino would pick Shamiq up every now and then when Wayne was in a good mood, and they'd cruise around in Wayne's Acura or Little Pacino's sixty-four Impala, and they'd pass bottles of Hennessy and E&J around and tell Shamiq war stories about how the three of them had hunted down kids who sang to the cops, dealers who turned informer. Shamiq tried to act like being around real crooks who sold crack and emptied clips at their enemies didn't faze him, and he hoped the older kids couldn't see the lump in his throat when they got drunk and showed off their stainless steel Rugers and Glocks.

Wayne must be taking this Claiborne for a ride. No other answer made sense. Shamiq hoped Wayne was being careful. But then, Wayne had never spent more than forty-eight hours in lockdown after that six-month stint in juvy for the gun possession when Shamiq was ten and Wayne was sixteen. Shamiq turned back to the mirror and began rehearsing his lines for the talent show.

A deep breath, a pause, another deep breath...

I pack big gats, push off coke crack and smack by the hundred pack and sit up late at night counting thousand-stacks, and offshore in the Caymans is where my money's at

I lived a lifetime of crime in these streets and I'm the best at what I do, And I wouldn't eye me up if I was you 'cause four fifths of my blood is straight Hennessy It be the fire in my veins that gives me energy, To aim, squeeze and cap out all my enemies, and cancel out the snitches who pretend to be Real players, but their masquerade is over when I approach.

Shit be for real, nigga, Big Wayne ain't no joke.

I'm the main man down in the Carolinas, Soon to be known from the east coast to Sidewinder, I got forty-five caliber snitch prevention, And been known to pop caps just for attention, Flippin' weight by the crate, state to state, The legacy of Super Hood the great..."

Shamiq smiled. His lyrics, based on Wayne's life, the closest he could come to the street without touching the cash or wearing the gold, had brought down the house at last year's talent show. The trophy still sat on the dresser, first place at age fourteen. Shamiq only wished he had a big flashy car like Wayne's, a crew of big-time distributors like the kids who sold for big bro, whom Wayne had promised to introduce him to when Shamiq was old enough to travel out of state with him. The phone rang again and the beep of the answering machine followed Wayne's message.

"Yeah, nigga," a young girl's voice said. She sounded about Shamiq's age. "Fuck was you at while I was at the hospital? I got the tests back. It ain't Tray Ball, and y'all the only two I was with that night. You don't talk to me tonight, I'm talking to the cops tomorrow. You over eighteen, remember?"

Beep.

Shamiq shook his head and laughed, looked from Wayne's picture to the mirror and resumed his lyrics.

"And these streets is packed full of coke-headed hoes and skanky tircks, scheming on the cash I pull down flipping solid white bricks, or yellowish cooked-up fifty-rocks, pushed off in out-of-state spots, try to say they pregnant so I'll spot 'em a hundred-knot, but my money stays mine, they can't take what I got..."

Shamiq popped in the instrumental tape he'd made with the drum machine and synthesizer his music teacher had loaned him, then hit play and record on a second tape player. He let a second or two pass, then started at the top. When he finished, he rewound the tape and timed himself. A minute and a half. Shamiq aimed for four or five, the average length of most of the rap songs he listened to. The judges last year had let each contestant go on for between three and six minutes, but Shamiq could go on for hours about Wayne's life out of state just on the strength of everything Wayne told him whenever he came home.

Wayne would sit on the dresser as Shamiq lay on the bottom bunk, a towel under the door if Mom was home, the window overlooking Eleventh cracked at the top and bottom to air out the room as Wayne puffed a blunt or a joint, swigging from the ever-present flask of Christian Brothers in the inside pocket of the leather Andrew marc coat or the three-quarter Nautica.

The phone rang again as Shamiq began to wonder where to begin his second verse, searching his mind for some particularly dramatic adventure Wayne might have recounted as the message played out and the machine beeped.

"Nigga, you must be crazy," a slurred voice Shamiq recognized as Little Pacino's said. "Me and Tray Ball just made bail, and I know you know why. I better either hear from you tonight or never see you again."

"Never scared, not even when old friends turn traitor, they'll see what's up when we meet up; and I cock back the slide and bring the heat up. They can talk shit but they can't come get me, 'cause I'll shoot up any punk that sweats me, as I make it to the top without a hitch, threaten me and you'll see payback's a bitch..."

Shamiq relished the cheers as he stepped on stage at William Penn. A couple of older girls in the front row blew him kisses as he took off Wayne's leather coat and lay it on the stool they'd provided under the single overhead spotlight. He gathered himself, aware of hundreds of eyes on him. Hair puffed out like Wayne's, gold chain and four-finger ring in place, Shamiq took the microphone from the mic-stand and nodded at his music teacher, offstage left, to start the beat. The bass thumped hard enough to make the stage vibrate under Shamiq's feet as the audience got to their feet and bobbed in time to the rhythm.

"What's up, William Penn!"

The crowd erupted into an encouraging roar, the sound of hands clapping echoed off the domed ceiling of the auditorium. Shamiq took a deep breath, let it out and and gripped the mic tighter.

"I pack big gats, push off coke, crack and smack by the hundred pack, and sit back late night counting thousand stacks..."

The next morning, Shamiq sat downstairs on the living room couch, watching the black-and-white TV. The image blurred and he got up to fix the aluminum foil on the broken antenna as he waited for his pop tarts to pop up in the kitchen/dining room. The high from the talent show had faded, even though another first-place trophy joined the one from last year on the dresser upstairs. Shamiq wondered again what Sheraton or Holiday Inn suite big bro was in. *The Enquirer* slid under the door as the toaster spat out Shamiq's pop tarts. Shamiq gave up struggling with the TV; no more of that once Wayne put him onto the coke game. No more Richard Allen, either. Outside, the neighborhood came to life as the first trolley rattled down the single set of rails on Eleventh. The smell of barbecue drifted across the street from someone's back grill.

Shamiq pictured big bro laying up on some waterbed, the Acura parked downstairs, suite air-conditioned with full cable service while Shamiq clicked on the rickety old fan in the front living room window and looked out at the grungy neighborhood he'd spent his whole life in. The ice-cream truck trundled up the pot-holed street, same as it did every Saturday morning, the neighbor's kids shot hoops in an orange crate up on a telephone pole, a couple of five-year-olds played in the hydrant on the corner of Eleventh and Diamond.

It wasn't fair, Shamiq thought, that his older brother could come and go as he pleased, while Shamiq couldn't even leave the house at night unless it was for the talent show or to head over to his cousin Greg's house on the West Side. Mom would call home from work to check on him, warning him he'd turn out like his big brother if he didn't stay in school. At least Wayne wasn't stuck here, losing his mind from the sameness of day-to-day life in the projects. Shamiq turned away from the window, grabbed his pop tarts and sat on the front steps with the paper, the day already hot, hazy and humid at eight AM.

What was the point of staying on the straight and narrow it this neighborhood was all he'd see for the next three years? Longer, if he didn't get a scholarship someplace, being as Philly Community College was for commuters only. Shamiq bit into his blueberry poptart, but the main headline killed his appetite.

But it had to be all lies. Easy when Wayne wasn't around to defend himself. But they'd interviewed kids who claimed they'd hustled with Wayne, who'd been locked up with him, and they'd all accused him of snitching. Could it be they were all jealous of big bro's status? Might be that the same was true of the girls who claimed Wayne had skipped out when they got back their EPT's.

Shamiq tried to square his image of the big brother he'd seen as Richard Allen's answer to Super Man with the news report.

Wayne had been the toughest thug in the projects. Never any fear in his eyes, always calm, come rain, sleet, snow or shell casings.

*Police found a three-gram bag of cocaine, a small amount of heroin and a bag of hypodermic syringes in the glove compartment of the decedent's vehicle...*

The newspaper photo showed Wayne in the Central Detention Center, six-two, two-ten, not a gram of body fat, ...*also a catalog of artificial growth hormones amid the bullet-riddled wreckage of the late-model Acura coupe registered to one* Darnell "Snake Eyes" Jenkins, *presently under indictment for a sweeping array of conspiracy charges...*

Shamiq sat Wayne's picture on the dresser with the rest of the family photos and looked in the mirror. After a moment, he started rhyming again, feeling weird without Wayne's jewelry or his jacket.

"I pack big gats, push off coke, crack and smack by the hundred-pack, and the long-sleeve Versace hides the needle tracks, and I scramble to pay all my debts back..."

Shamiq hung his own picture where Wayne's had been and turned back to the mirror, noticing for the first time how fast his peach-fuzz mustache was growing in.

"I'm out of the shadow of Super Hood. A little heart, a lot of luck and I'll make it all super good I got brains even if I ain't got muscle, And who says I gotta get 'em blown out in some drug tussle?"

**Steve Dimeo**
**Hillsboro, OR**

## Going through Umbrellas

I seem to go through umbrellas
the way those ghostly cancer cells
storm through your good blood.

Exasperated with two black ones whose
worn tines droop like limp bat wings,
I've bought another cheaper small
device with an automatic opener,
hoping that this will better weather
the endless rainy seasons here
and the trials I put them through.

Small enough for me to stuff
into the pocket of this parka
you bought me for Christmas
where I hopefully won't forget
it as I have others before,
it doesn't fully cover much more
than my head and shoulders.
When the winds slant the rain enough,
nothing much prevents the rest
of me from getting wet.

Content with older, frailer favorites,
forgetting a moment my fear
that this won't last much longer
either than the other ones did—
maybe a year or two at best
before in my haste to mushroom the cover
I may tear a hole here or there—
I finally raise this flimsy shield
against the fallen dawn.

Sometimes, though, I think I prefer
just to walk without an umbrella at all,
knowing that, rain tearing from my hood,
I can still get back home again
soaked outside, desert-dry within,
            shorn at the prospect of losing you
as I shamble my way alone into morning.

# Gnomon

Cleaning off the back patio
prior to turning under the flower
garden you never finished before
I'll seed it with more grass instead,
I unearth the sundial you bought
for us so many years ago.
Time has changed it some,
lending it a verdigris patina,
bending its gnomon, too,
maybe from the same ice storm
that toppled our butterfly tree
and marked the downturn
in our fight against your leukemia.

But what I notice most are Browning's words
that wreathe the image of Father Time
shouldering his lethal scythe:
"Grow old along with me,
The best is yet to be."

Choking on my own breath,
I bring the dial to the plastic seat
of faux marble near our bird feeders,
set it at one corner, and try to position
the gnomon so that it points north
as its shadow slashes across the "V."

The slanted gnomon angles above
the butterflied wings of a phoenix
towards the cloud-smeared blue
of the sky over our dream home
and where I imagine Polaris is,
the center that cannot hold
for this new reeling universe.

Without you, the gnomon's homonym
identifies exactly what I've become
no man nothing now without you.

Eastward still its peak crooks,
a finger hooked towards where
the sun should rise narrow tomorrow
when this dial will register
only the twilight of my heart.

## Used Book Display

I man the booth of used books
at every summer Sunday market,
volunteering for the local library
because I think that's what
they say I'm supposed to do
after so suddenly losing you.

But I feel as I try to visit
with the periodic passers-by
who mostly stop in to look,
a few buying some paperbacks
the library no longer needs,
that *I'm* the one on display
like a freak for playful pillory,
as though I wear an unseen
sign over my damaged chest:
here sits a man just retired
who lost his wife to cancer,
bereft, trying in vain again
to reconnect with an outside
world of others who think
this can't happen to them.

I believe I'm more like a creature
behind a zoo's invisible bars
like Yeats' circus animal deserted
meant to entertain the rest
with a little *Schadenfreude* —
the "bad joy" that will make
them feel lucky and secure
that I'm the only one here
who failed to finish a volume
you and I shared for a lifetime,
discarded for resale too soon.

*Deborah Gorman*
*St. John, IN*

# Cornerstone Church

It was a glorious Sunday morning, the late August sun a blazing eye in a vast sea of blueness, high clouds reminiscent of fish scales and long strips of chaste rippled sand. The previous day had been hot and humid, oppressive air heavy with pollen, dust and other pollutants. But brief mid-night showers purified the skies, a heavenly eraser wiping the atmosphere clean. Though the heat was still there, it was much more tolerable.

Cassie's car windows were rolled all the way down so she could enjoy the breeze. If traffic was light on these country roads during normal rush hour, on Sundays it was almost non-existent. At the moment there was hardly anyone out besides the few souls going either to the Speedway for gas or a newspaper, or to church. Cassie was among the latter.

The Cornerstone Church, her destination, had mailed her a postcard the week before. While not exactly mailed to her personally, the exciting announcement that "There is a **new church** in your **community!**" invited "Postal Patron" to come and check it out. "We have a passion to spread the good news of the gospel with deeds of mercy," it read. And both website and physical addresses were accompanied by a map.

As it just so happened that she was in the market for a church to attend regularly, and it just so happened that this was her favored denomination, and it just so happened to be less than a five-mile drive from her house, Cassie decided to go there after visiting their impressive website. It seemed almost that she was *being sent* there.

After a couple of wrong turns despite the map, she found it bounded on three sides by towering corn, a brand new red brick Colonial structure topped with a tall slender white steeple. The parking lot in front was not yet finished; a guardian troop of orange sandbags mounted atop striped sawhorses shielded freshly-poured cement curbs from trespassers.

The lot was nowhere near full to capacity, with maybe fifteen late-model cars and SUVs lined up in only the first two rows. A beat up old bicycle lay, unhitched, beneath a recently planted tree still wearing a yellow plastic tag around its trunk. Walking away from it toting a big Bible, was a thirty-something guy dressed in jeans and a bright Hawaiian shirt.

Cassie swung into the canyon between a white Explorer and a black Escalade, and checked the time on her dashboard clock. Nine-twenty-nine. Though the couple of wrong turns had delayed her, services began at nine-thirty and it wouldn't take a whole minute to get inside. She didn't want to make a bad first impression by being late, tardiness might seem disrespectful. On her hurried way to the double front doors, she spotted the "2002" etched into the cornerstone—this building hadn't been here a year.

The foyer was empty save for a large circular table displaying an assortment of papers, and books. Beyond it was another set of double doors leading to the sanctuary. A glass partition between the two areas revealed the sanctuary itself, its long rows of oaken pews halved by a wide aisle carpeted in a shade of gray. Just inside the doors, a suited fortyish man and a perhaps-fifteen-year-old boy were engaged in conversation. As Cassie approached, the man disengaged to seat himself, leaving the usher alone to usher.

She entered the sanctuary and said good morning to the boy who merely echoed her. While waiting for him to part with a bulletin from the bundle he held in both hands, she surveyed the room from right to left. When he said nothing and didn't move, she wondered if he might need some prompting. "Are those the programs you're holding?" she asked.

"Uh huh," he said flatly.

"May I have one?" She extended her hand.

When he still didn't move, she just reached down and took one. *Like pulling teeth,* she thought. Then, having already chosen a center aisle seat in an almost empty row near the back, she sat down on the "bride's side." One young couple was seated directly in front of her and another was directly behind.

As it turned out, she wasn't even close to being late. In fact, she had time enough to read the bulletin twice in addition to studying the features of both the church's architecture and attendants.

The design was simple and unpretentious, walls and windows relatively non-descript, pews upholstered in solid royal blue. The lower portion of front wall that was paneled behind the altar had two disguised doors, betrayed only by unobtrusive door handles. Due to their intended invisibility, a person almost had to know they were there to know they were there.

On one side of the altar was a modest communion table and on the other a baptismal font. In the center was the minister's lectern and behind all was a very large pipe organ. It occupied the whole upper portion of the front wall. Curiously, though the organist was already playing, the music sounded as though it were in no way coming through those pipes. Cassie wondered whether there was some kind of bypass system or a volume control; judging by the size of the pipes, the music they were listening to should be a lot bigger and louder. Maybe that was something they saved only for holidays or other special occasions, she thought.

The small congregation sat patiently waiting, with very little whispering or talking going on. Except for the guy in the Hawaiian shirt, all of the men were wearing suits and ties. She wouldn't know what the women were wearing until everyone stood up. As she scanned the backs of peoples' heads, something seemed different about this group. Whether it was something already here that she wasn't seeing, or something that wasn't here that should have been, she couldn't tell.

Despite the abundance of vacant space in the pews, she felt the presence of God. Strangely she didn't feel it in every church. If someone ever asked her to describe the intangible sensation of God's presence, she knew it would be impossible. She only knew when she felt it, or when she didn't. Because she felt it in this church, she knew this one definitely had it.

Suddenly the service appeared to be starting. The music ended as a man in a blue suit stepped up to the lectern. "Good morning," he said, and there was silence.

"I'd like to remind you that after our evening service tonight, we'll be having our book discussion. If you don't have the book we've been discussing on the subject of marriage, we have plenty of copies to spare. Just please sign up this morning on the back table and we'll reserve one for you.

"Also on the back table is a sign-up sheet for side dishes and desserts for the church picnic the Saturday following Labor Day. That would be September 6 in case you want to mark your calendar. We'll have a short meeting in the Hearthside Room after this morning's service for anyone willing to help out.

"I'm sure you'll be happy to know that our website is up and running again. We had a few minor problems with that, but we're confident that everything's straightened out now. Check out our discussion board there, and we have audio files and archived copies of past sermons and bulletins. And I encourage you to direct people interested in learning about our church to our website. We want to spread the good word."

The announcements dragged on for a good ten minutes as he covered Council meetings and church directory pictures, upcoming car washes and camping trips; things that were already in the bulletin. The one thing he didn't say was "Welcome," at least for the benefit of anonymous Postal Patrons —and in this half-empty place, they should stand out like black sheep among white.

After a prayer there was a hymn for which everyone stood confirmation that all of the women were wearing dresses. The high school age girls were wearing dresses as well, though high school age boys were a little more casual in dress slacks and collared shirts. As the only woman wearing slacks and a short-sleeved blouse, Cassie supposed she was on the same par as the guy in the Hawaiian shirt, sitting way up front also by himself.

Another hymn and another prayer; a very long one that included everything. This was the Congregational Prayer asking for the comfort of specific members who were sick, and the strength to deal with sin in a sinful world. It also acknowledged God's many blessings, "excellent nursing homes" named among them.

*That's what it is!* thought Cassie. Her eyes sprang open and she scanned heads again, seeking to calculate the median age here. While the youngest were infants maybe days or weeks old, the oldest couldn't have exceeded early forties. That these people represented a mere two generations was odd; and there wasn't a gray hair in sight.

He continued to pray. "We ask that You take special care of Andrea, Nicole, Rebecca, Susan and Julie —our pregnant moms— and take special care of the babes in their wombs. And please look after the children, Lord. Look after the children…"

If they had more than the many present, some couples sure did have plenty of them!

"We are sinners, Lord, but forgive us. In just this past week we have made ourselves drunk with alcohol and we have been gluttons with food. We have watched pornography on television and in movies, allowing our eyes to see and ears to hear things they shouldn't have seen or heard. We have spent far more money than we can afford to spend on material things, putting our families in debt. We have coveted our neighbors' belongings and have committed adultery against our spouses…"

*Hey, wait just a minute!* thought Cassie. She had enough legitimate sins to account for already without admitting guilt for sins she hadn't even committed! She didn't want him praying on her behalf if this was what he had in mind but, when she looked around for evidence that somebody agreed with her, no one else seemed to have a problem with it.

"And, Father, protect us and protect our marriages. Protect us from this sinful world, protect us from evil. Protect our children, our spouses and our families. We need your protection, Lord…"

He dwelled on this, asking for so much of it, especially for their marriages, it gave the impression that they considered everyone and everything a threat. Finally he ran out of requests.

"We ask this in the precious name of Jesus Christ. Amen."

She took a deep breath and blew it out slowly, grateful to say amen to *that!* Now it was time for the offering.

Cassie searched for a Visitor Card, the kind usually stored with the hymnals and Bibles which, here, were in the tray beneath the pew in front of her. She'd print her name and address, and maybe check the box that said she had come in response to their postcard. They probably kept track of that stuff.

But there were no Visitor Cards. When a man in a gray suit came by with the collection plate, she just smiled and shook her head.

They sang another hymn.

To follow the reading of scripture, Cassie used the Bible from the tray. Its pages were still so crisp and stiff, she thought she must be the first person to turn them. The blue-suited man read Psalm 15 aloud:

*"Lord, who may dwell in your sanctuary? Who may live on your holy hill? He whose walk is blameless and who does what is righteous, who speaks the truth from his heart and has no slander on his tongue, who does his neighbor no wrong and casts no slur on his fellowman, who despises a vile man but honors those who fear the Lord, who keeps his oath even when it hurts, who lends his money without usury and does not accept a bribe against the innocent. He who does these things will never be shaken."*

Evidently the man was the pastor because he also delivered the sermon, an expository of the scripture he'd read. Though his beginning was somewhat weak, he improved as he got deeper into it. Cassie especially liked what he had to say about the importance of keeping one's word:

"When you make a promise to someone, God wants you to keep it no matter what. Just like He always does! That's what we're talking about here, about a man who keeps his oath even when it hurts.

"Let's say that you're in the construction business, and a customer asks you for a price on a job. So you quote him a price. Then suddenly your cost for material or labor goes up. Do you go back to the customer and say, 'Sorry, but I have to raise my price'?

"No, you keep your oath even when it hurts. When God sees you keep your word at your own expense, that's what makes Him happy."

And Cassie didn't doubt that at all.

After the sermon there were but a few brief moments of formality before the pastor closed the service. Then, head lowered, he walked down the center aisle toward the sanctuary doors, eyes focused on the carpet just in front of him. Ordinary organ music started again while people gathered their things, preparing to exit. Herding into the aisle, they faced the back of the room where Cassie stood waiting for someone to let her cut in, or at least to acknowledge her.

Not a single one did.

Although indeed several locked eyes with her, none used it as an opening when she smiled at them. When they simply looked away, Cassie couldn't account for it.

She glanced over their approaching heads at the paneled doors, at the unobtrusive door handles, and wondered whether her presence was equally as difficult to detect. But, no, that couldn't be it.

Her attention returned to those exiting as she still stood waiting for someone —who?—anyone, to say something! "Good morning" perhaps, or "I'm so glad you came," or "Welcome to our cornfield." Anything!

But nothing. From no one. *Like livestock,* she thought sadly. *Like animals with no free will.*

By the time the guy in the Hawaiian shirt made eye contact with her, she was so disgusted all she wanted was to get out of there. As soon as he passed by, she surged in behind him without even asking to be excused. When she was almost to the sanctuary doors, the pastor reached out to shake her hand, skipping the Hawaiian shirt guy altogether.

"Good morning," Cassie managed lamely.

"Good morning," said the pastor. And he quickly went on to the next person as she was processed into the foyer.

*Well, at least he saw me,* she thought, wondering how she could have felt God's presence in this place.

The herd was going somewhere in particular, a smaller side room off the foyer. Cassie took a peek for curiosity's sake. A table was nicely laid-out with trays of donuts, cookies and coffee. That's what was so important?

Giving everybody one final chance to communicate, she stalled at the foyer table pretending to be interested in the literature on it. Except there was no literature on it, just sign-up sheets for different activities, and the books about marriage. She sighed and walked slowly to the front doors, digging her car keys out of the bottom of her purse.

Outside three men stood together under the building's carport, the guy in the Hawaiian shirt walking away from them. The three not even talking to each other seemed only to be standing alone together as a group. Cassie wondered if, while their wives were busy eating donuts, they were forbidden to even speak with other men. She watched as the Hawaiian shirt guy turned back to take one more look at them and just kept walking.

The interior of the car was so hot, Cassie opened all the windows and vents before backing out of her parking space. As she wound her way to the exit, she saw the Hawaiian shirt guy already hiking along the country road, toting his Bible, in the direction that she was headed. But hadn't he come here on a bicycle?

She stepped on the brake and backed up several yards so she could see the base of the tree where it had been. The bike was gone.

But who would have taken it, locked or unlocked? Not only could she not picture someone stealing such an old beat up bike. Way out here in the middle of cornfields, who else but she had known he'd in fact left it there? Would someone have followed him just to take it while he was inside the church? That was unlikely, yet irrelevant at this point anyway. What was relevant was, how far did he have to walk and why had those three men not helped him?

Cassie shifted the car into gear and left the property, slowly pulling up behind him on the road's shoulder. He didn't respond though he had to have heard her tires crunching the gravel. "Excuse me," she yelled as she got out.

He stopped and turned around. When he smiled his whole face changed somehow, and Cassie felt a kind of warmth she'd never experienced before, right down to her DNA. She also felt a strange kind of recognition, something she couldn't quite put her finger on. She definitely knew him from somewhere, or had at least seen or met him someplace before. Occupied with searching her memory for a clue, it was hard to compose an intelligible sentence.

"I saw . . . I mean, I noticed that you . . .your bike was under the tree this morning and you were but now..." She stopped to slap her own cheek. "I'm sorry. I should think for a second."

He laughed. She sighed.

"Okay. Do you need a ride somewhere?"

"Just to the Speedway," he said.

With a grand sweep of her arm, she invited him into her car. Regrettably she had to keep her eyes on the road when she'd much rather look at him. With the gas station only three miles away, this favor would be accomplished in less than five minutes, perhaps not enough time to remember where she knew him from.

"I can't imagine what happened to your bike."

When he didn't answer, she thought perhaps he'd rather not discuss it.

"Are you a regular at that church?" she said.

"I've never been there before."

"Me either. So what did you think?"

"I'd be more interested to hear what you think," he said.

Cassie wasn't exactly sure what to think. "Hmm, I'd have to say that I didn't like it."

He looked at her expectantly, as if he wanted details.

"Well, I felt invisible, like nobody even knew I was there." She tried to gauge his non-reaction. "You must have felt that way, too, like nobody saw you."

"You saw me."

"I'm talking about the rest of those people. It was like we were both invisible or something. How could I be invisible? Or you? Especially in that shirt? I mean, no offense to your shirt or your taste in clothes. I just mean that it stands out, it begs to be noticed. But that minister didn't just *not* shake your hand, he ignored you! And those three men outside— I saw them do the same thing!"

"But you didn't ignore me."

"Yeah, but we're not talking about me."

"Aren't we?"

Cassie was confused and yet she wasn't. What those people had done to both of them wasn't right, in fact, it was downright un-Christian! Yet someone had at least acknowledged her with a handshake, insufficient welcome as it was. That they had rudely ignored and neglected this man was inexcusable, and she was angry and ashamed to have mistaken them for brethren.

"I'm Cassie and I'm happy to meet you," she said hoping it could make up for something.

"Cassie, I'm very glad to know you. And I thank you for your kindness to me."

It felt wrong for her to accept thanks, however. From childhood she'd been taught that an act of kindness was its own reward, the satisfaction coming not in the form of gratitude from the act's recipient, but from simply knowing that the act had been done.

"Do you remember the second greatest commandment?" he said.

"The second commandment? Oh gosh, let me think. Is it— "

"No, not the second commandment. The second *greatest* commandment. Do you remember what that is?"

She knew but what was it again? Think. Think!

"The greatest commandment," he reminded her, "is to love the Lord your God with all your heart and with all your soul and with all your mind and with all your strength. And the second?"

"Um, to love your neighbor as yourself?"

"Yes, you are exactly right."

And there was the Speedway on the busiest corner of nowhere, the place where they would part company. Cassie was still unable to remember where she knew him from.

Pulling onto the drive, she carefully navigated through the pumps on her way up the incline to the building. She stopped near the door, putting the car into Park so the locks would open automatically. He took hold of the door handle and hesitated. "Do you remember what Jesus said about the sheep and the goats?"

"Not off the top of my head, no."

"When Jesus returns in his glory, he will separate the sheep from the goats, putting the sheep on his right and the goats on his left. Then he will say to those on his right, 'Only you will join me in my kingdom because you are blessed because you fed me when I was hungry, you gave me something to drink when I was thirsty, you invited me in when I was a stranger, you clothed me when I needed clothes, you nursed me when I was sick and you visited me in prison.'

"And they will say, 'Lord, but how can that be, when we have never met you face to face before?' Now you remember, don't you, Cassie? Tell me, how does it end?"

"Then he'll say, 'If you did these things for the least of my brothers, you did them for me.'"

"Yes, you did them for me." And then he smiled again, bringing her the same feeling of warmth she'd felt a few minutes before, an intangible feeling she couldn't have described had someone asked her to do so.

"You never did tell me your name," she said.

"There's no need. You already know me."

"I do? I mean, I do! But I. . ."

"And don't worry. You'll see me again. I promise." Then he got out and shut the door.

She watched him enter the building, frantically sifting through her mental files for some hint that might reveal who he was or how she knew him. But the answer just wouldn't materialize. Perhaps she was trying too hard right now; it would probably come to her later once she stopped thinking about it.

At the bottom of the incline when she stepped on the brake, something slid out from under the passenger seat. *Oh no!* she thought, *his Bible!* He must have set it by his feet when he sat down and it had been swallowed in the uphill climb. Quickly she turned the car around and went back up the incline, hoping to catch him before he caught another ride.

Inside the building where customers paid for their gas, a lone clerk sat behind the counter reading a newspaper. Country music played in the background. Cassie ran to the center of the room and did a 360-degree turn.

"Hi, can I help you with something?" said the clerk.

"Yes, I'm looking for the guy in the Hawaiian shirt."

The clerk look confused. "What guy? When was he here?"

"I just dropped him off a couple minutes ago. He left something in my car that I have to return to him. Do you know where he went?"

The clerk looked around the room and then shrugged. "If he came in here, I didn't see him."

"Well, I don't know how you could have missed him! Unless there's another door to this place and he just walked right through."

"Nope, only one door. If you saw him come in and didn't see him come out, he'd still be here. I think you're mistaken."

No, she wasn't mistaken! He did walk through that door and this Bible belonged to him! Or was that not real, either? She'd find out here and now. "Can I ask you one more thing?"

"Sure."

"What am I holding in my hand?"

"Huh?"

"Just tell me what you see in my hand."

The clerk leaned forward for a closer look. "A Bible would be my guess."

Well, at least *that* wasn't invisible!

Cassie got back in the car laughing at the absurdity of the whole situation, amazed at having experienced such a morning. None of it made any sense at all, and she seemed to be the only witness. But she had to find a way to return this Bible.

Setting it on her lap, she leafed through it in search of something with his name on it. While a postcard addressed to "Postal Patron" wouldn't tell her who he was, it would give her an honest lead.

There was nothing.

Remembering that big Bibles customarily have pages reserved for important family dates, like births, deaths and marriages, she checked to see if this one had them. It did, but they were still blank.

Running out of ideas, she went all the way back to the beginning, starting with the inside of the front cover. Nothing. But when she turned to the bookplate on the next page, what she saw sucked the breath right out of her.

There were three lines available for owner information, preceded by the words "Presented to." And on the top line, in a beautiful calligraphy, was the name "Cassie Hayward," which was impossible. Cassie Hayward wasn't *his* name, it was *her* name! How did *her* name get into *his* Bible? How could? how was. . .? how did he. . .?

On the second line was "blessed and beloved."

Suddenly the magnitude of it hit her like a meteor, and a flash of heat filled her with joy. She rested her head on the steering wheel and began to cry, finally aware of who he was.

And in that moment she realized that she could go home now, since she wouldn't see him again today. But she did know that she'd see him again *someday*- because he had given her His Word.

*Steve Dimeo*
*Hillsboro, OR*

## Feting by the Black Willamette

Lit from within like our new Christmas tree
with its built-in fiber optic stem and limbs
spinning slowly in a twinkling dance,
we feted this fateful day the news
that your new diet and the mild chemo
had dropped the cancer cells and raised
the count of neutrophils that could
help you fight off your plague of sores.

Dressed in your short burgundy velvet
Victoria's Secret dress, you held my arm
as we went to our favorite restaurant
on Swan Island that overlooked the black
waters of the Willamette River stippled
with the white lights of a saurian derrick
stretching above steel chaos across from us.
We dined on our favorite meals
me my salmon, you your rare steak
talking of all we had yet to dream
of in our first month of retirement as
we watched tugboats swan their way
over gentle ripples of a dark river
reflecting city lights like silvery fingerlings,
vibrant stars wriggling wakes for us to follow.

At evening's end the hostess snapped our picture
before the simply decorated tree in the foyer,
your dress playing off the burgundy turtleneck
I'd covered with the white sweater vest
you'd knitted for me and the gray jacket

you gave me the Christmas before.
You pressed your ring-fingered hand
against my chest while I touched your wrist,
neither of us wanting now to let go,
swan lights behind us haloing our smiles.

Even in the midst of the black waters
that overwhelmed us and still me,
I remember us in that hopeful pose
as one recalls smolts glittering downstream
towards an ever darker sea.

*Tessa Nelson-Humphries*
*Las Cruces NM*

## Middle-Aged Math Prof Thinks He's Archimedes' Screw!

After demonstrating chords and polyhedrons
Adulterous middle-aged B made elementary proposition
To homely A, his student.
Soon, equipotentially, they merged on an inclined plane.
Avoided multiplying, so Zero-Population growth.
But this elliptical relationship soon became third-class
When acute B constructed a tangent
Back to his cone-headed spouse C,
Polarised in their split-level cube,
Squarely-rooted, unaware of the base problem
And its increasing differential.
But gossip multiplied.
The Dean deduced B's sum
Was minus intrinsic value
And fired him, fractionated.

\* \* \*

## Racing Towards A Supermarket Shelf in Silks

Hundredweights of horseflesh
Thunder down tracks from the far turn,
Nostrils flaring, eyes bloodshot.
On glossy backs hunch wizened gnomes
Sweating through gaudy silks - purple, orange,
Duck-merde green, blood-red.
Leather-faced tiny trolls

Beat, curse, slash, flog flesh along the stretch run.

As goaded beasts blur by in the sport of kings
Mindless mobs mouth and roar.
Greedy for blood-money howl hard-faced harridans in hideous hats
Race run, some solon shrouds
The trembling winner in blood-red roses
Before handing a chased urinal
Taller than the
Mounted midget mugging and whip-waving.

Equine champ, for a while,
Will crop bluegrass behind white fences
When not being goaded into mounting skittish mares
While stunted stableboys scream smut.
It's the losers they should scream for,
Broken-winded, spavined, lamed,
Yet still life-loving.
But no bluegrass, coy mares, careful currying for them.

Their prize for 'failure' is a filthy slaughterhouse.
A final flogging along tracks slimed with bloody guts
Before being shackled, hoisted, skinned to bloody pulp
And ground up for pet food
Or dinner for the elderly poor. A stat not in the Studboook!
Their reward for racing their guts out in gaudy silks
Is to be coffined in a can
And catacombed on supermarket shelves.

*Bruce Henricksen*
*Duluth, MN*

## Where the Road Ends

*daylight*

The road ends in ruts and stones
Where an ancient barn sinks
Back in grass.

A dog rests, chin on paws,
Dreaming of voices
And hands.

Weeds clutch broken glass
And shotgun shells.
The moon

Emerges from a fading
Pool of light, and
A hawk turns

In wind untangled
From aspen and pine.
The twilight

## Leaks away, drainage from a pond.

*evening*

The bending branches squeak
Like corks in wine bottles
Held close in alleys.

The whistle of a distant train
Is a violin yearning,
And the dog

Howls his same old canine blues
Then stops to search for
Someplace warm.

Under the moon, the old dirt
Road is a graying
Bone.

Clouds unfold and turn to scraps
that race beneath the sky
And stars.

The night is wild with wings and eyes.

* * *

## My Mother Dies

Her breathing comes and goes
Like wind that rests in
Fields on farms.

Small things sing in summer air.

The sounds receding from her room
Are birds that flow on currents
Down a ridge.

She sees strange alphabets
Of shadow in
The grass.

The light is less. She dreams
Of cattle gathering
Toward a barn.

Leaves turn faces toward the ground
And change to stones along
A riverbed.

* * *

## In Some Far and Other Time

When the reds and browns of this
October day are rearranged
By memory, what shades and hues
Will myth select for us? Will you
Recall a me in black and white,
And I a sepia-tinted you?

In some far and other time
What liberties will autumn take?
Will the lake still drift from lime
To blue when age has dimmed the sky,
And will the sunset pour itself
Upon the shore like fruit and wine?

What portraits of ourselves will line
The walls that time is yet to build?
Will the pictured eyes betray
Amazement at our emerald bay?
How will the colors of the now
Have changed when it is yesterday?

*Fred Zachau*
*Oakdale MN*

# The Rattlesnake, the Bull, and the Nation

For some time now one of my goals in life has been to climb to the highest point in every state. All I do is climb up, look around, say, "Wow," take a few photos, and then climb back down, but I get a certain satisfaction out of each climb. The higher the peak and the more challenging the climb, the greater the satisfaction. Sir Edmund Hilary would understand.

Just before Labor Day a couple of Septembers ago, I hiked to the summit of Wheeler Peak, the highest point in New Mexico. Although there's a story to this Wheeler Peak hike, it's not the one I'm going to tell now. This story is about my trip back home to Minnesota after Wheeler Peak. My plan was to hike to the highest elevations in Nebraska, South Dakota, and North Dakota along the way. There's nothing really challenging about these three hikes, or so I thought, but I decided that I'd pick them up just for completeness.

I flunked Nebraska. I couldn't find the highest point. It was marked on the map I had as just south of I-80 right on the Colorado border near the Oliver Reservoir Recreation Area. I got off the freeway and pulled into the recreation area, which was jammed with people swimming, fishing, boating, picnicking, and camping, and I asked some of them how to get to the state's highest point. None of them knew. In fact, most of them were surprised that it was in this part of the state. I finally located a ranger who worked in the recreation area and asked him.

"Oh, sure," he said, "it's over south of the freeway."

"Yeah, but how do I get there?"

He then confessed that he had never been there. It was on or near one of those gravel roads over that way, but he wasn't sure just which one. The highest point in Nebraska is apparently not one of the state's great tourist attractions. Nebraska would have to wait until some other time. I gave up and drove on to the Black Hills. The next day I hiked to the top of Harney Peak, the tallest peak in South Dakota. This is a very easy, very pretty hike, only six miles round trip. The only bad part was that since it was the day before Labor Day, the trail was so crowded that it was more like standing in a checkout line in a supermarket than hiking through a peaceful woods. That afternoon I drove on to the town of Amidon, North Dakota.

As far as I can tell, the town of Amidon has three distinguishing attributes. First, it is the smallest county seat in the United States; it has a population of twenty-four. Second, it is the closest town to White Butte, the highest point in North Dakota. Third, although it has no cop, it does have a police car. The townsfolk came up with a late model car that looked pretty good, but had a blown engine, painted the car white, added the word "Police" in large blue letters on each front door, screwed a red light on the roof, and placed a dummy, who wears a highway patrolman's hat, behind the wheel. The car is permanently parked along the road at the edge of town. I spotted it just in time to get under Amidon's speed limit via panic breaking.

When I got to the other side of town—it only took a matter of seconds—I decided to go back and ask the cop for directions to White Butte. I pulled up next to his car and looked in. I could see him sitting behind the wheel. He didn't move. Looked like he fell asleep. Well, it's a pretty dull job, just sitting there watching traffic go by. I raced my engine and pulled up closer. He still didn't move. A sound sleeper. I looked in and saw the terrible gray pallor on his face. My god, he's dead. Probably killed by an irate motorist. I got out of my car and ran to his window. A dummy, a mannequin. Crap. I drove to one of Amidon's two stores and told the proprietor about my experience with their local policeman.

"Yup," he drawled, "He don't give out too much infermashun, but he sure slows down them there speeders."

"Well, he sure slowed me down. Tell me, how do I get to White Butte?"

"Every once in a while somebody stops by and asks me that, so I drew up a map." He handed me a copy. "The butte's on private land. Before ya go up there, stop at the owner's place and ask her permission. She'll say it's okay. Her house is on the map. Oh, and by the way, ya see on the map right near the foot of the butte that area I got marked 'snake dens?' Lots of rattlers in there. They got nests down in the rocks. I marked it on the map 'cause a few folks been bit there."

"Oh, okay, well, uh, thanks." I followed the directions on the map: two miles east of Amidon on the highway, then five miles south on a gravel road, and finally another mile west on another gravel road. The owner turned out to be a very pleasant elderly lady who owned a small friendly dog. (I had imagined being greeted by a huge farm dog whose favorite sport was chewing on the calves of visitors.) The owner was not unhappy to see me. I guessed that life is a little lonesome out there near White Butte.

"Oh, yes, you may climb up there. Just follow the road that runs along that fence line until you come to another fence line. At the corner there you'll find a gate. Go through the gate and you'll be at the foot of the butte. But watch out for rattlesnakes."

I assured her I would. "I see a lot of cows out there," I said. "There isn't a bull mixed in with those cows, is there?"

"Well, yes, there is a bull, but I don't think he's up on the butte. I saw him down here at the other end of the field earlier this morning. But he won't bother you. If you leave him alone, he'll leave you alone."

At this point I have to explain that I'm not a country boy. I was born, raised, and lived all my life in the city, except for the summer of 1958. In 1958 I had a scholarship from the Magnolia Petroleum Company (now a part of ExxonMobil) at the University of Minnesota. Along with the scholarship went a summertime job working on one of Magnolia's seismic parties prospecting for oil in the area around Roswell, New Mexico, an area with a large population of both rattlesnakes and cattle. It was there that I learned not to be afraid to hike in rattlesnake country. I learned that rattlesnakes seldom attack, that if you make a small amount of noise when you walk and give them a chance to get away, they will. I spent that entire summer walking around in rattlesnake country near Roswell and have since been hiking in parts of California and Arizona, which have a high rattlesnake density, and have seen rattlesnakes only infrequently, and those that I have seen were hurrying away as fast as they could.

To explain how I learned about cows and bulls, I first have to give a quick explanation of how a seismic party operated back in 1958. I don't know how they operate now; I never worked in the field after I got out of school and haven't tried to keep up with the technology. But here's how they operated in 1958.

The first crew to come along was the drilling crew. This crew would drill a shallow hole in the ground, place a small charge of dynamite in the hole, and then cover it up leaving only a copper wire sticking out of the ground. They'd also stick a red flag next to the hole so the next crew could find it. Then a second crew would come along and lay out long cables on the ground in a radial pattern near the dynamite hole. About every ten or fifteen feet along each of the long cables was a connector to which the crew would attach a geophone. A geophone is like a microphone except it picks up vibrations in the solid earth instead of sound vibrations in the air.

The third crew had the seismograph in a truck. This crew would attach each of the long cables with the geophones to the seismograph and then set off the dynamite charge. The vibrations from the explosion would be reflected off any discontinuities between different types of rock down in the earth—for example, the discontinuity formed where a layer of sandstone overlies a layer of shale. At these interfaces some of the vibration energy would be reflected back to the surface, and the geophones would pick up these reflections and pass them on to the seismograph, which would record them. Back in the office a skilled seismologist would read the seismograms and draw a picture of the underground structural geology of the area. We were looking for salt domes because in that area around Roswell salt domes often contained oil. The last crew to come along would pick up the cables. I often worked on this crew.

Cattle, I learned, are curious animals. Quite often between the time the seismograph crew left and the cable-pickup crew arrived, cattle would wander over to see what was going on. We would often find them standing around amongst the cables, standing on the cables, and lying down on the cables. Most of the cattle were the white face beef cattle that you still see so many of out west. Except for me and one other student and the boss, the regulars on the seismic crew were all ex-cowboys who had discovered that they could make more money prospecting for oil than they could punching cows. They taught me that these white face cattle are a gentle breed. You could usually chase them away simply by yelling and waving your hat in the air. Even the bulls are surprisingly gentle.

Back in 1958 there were still a few Texas longhorns roaming the range. Some ranchers kept them out of nostalgia. Others, as tourist attractions. The cowboys forgot to tell me that these longhorns have a different temperament from the whitefaces. One day I made the mistake of yelling and waving my hat a longhorn bull. Instead of running away, he chased me back to the truck. Very funny to the cowboys, but not to me. (I later learned that they were really concerned for my safety until I leaped into the truck bed.) That bull instilled in me a fear of bulls—I don't care what kind of bull it is—that lives with me today.

I left the owner's house, got into my pickup, and drove to the corner of the two fence lines where the gate was located. I went through the gate, walked carefully through the area of snake dens, and climbed up one of the two paths I saw to what seemed to be the highest point of the butte. At first I thought that the paths were human paths maybe made by hikers, but they weren't. They were cow paths. On top of the butte I found cows, about twenty or thirty of them. And cow pies, about two or three thousand of them. I had trouble finding the highpoint marker. Could it be under a cow pie? I refuse to tramp around picking up cow pies to find it. Just after making this decision, I saw it.

I took a few photos and started down the other cow path. The climb up the butte is quiet gentle except for the first forty or fifty feet, which are very steep. Over these forty or fifty feet, the path that I was on got so steep that I took a different route down. After I got to the bottom I looked up and was amazed to see the twenty or thirty cows all in single file working their way down this very steep path. I had no idea that cows are so sure-footed. They were jogging down the path that was too steep for me, and I mean jogging. The path was too steep for them to walk down. After they got to the bottom, they single-filed their way toward the owner's house. I got at the end of the line and followed. Except, they didn't go to the house. They stopped at the corner of the fence lines where the gate was located, the gate I had to go through to get to my truck.

As I approached them I waved my hat in the air and yelled, "Okay, Ladies, move it. I've got to get out the gate." And I whooped my best cowboy whoop, which probably wasn't very good; I don't believe I'd whooped since 1958. But it worked. They all trotted a short distance away and then turned around and looked at me. All of them, that is, except one very large white cow, which was standing right next to the gate, almost touching it. When I got to within about twenty feet of this very large white cow, I noticed that a certain appendage was missing and in its place was a different appendage. It was, of course, the bull.

The picture of the longhorn chasing me flashed through my mind. I didn't whoop or wave my hat in the air. I considered saying, "Sir Bull, would you mind moving about ten or fifteen paces to your right so I can get out the gate?" but decided it wouldn't do any good. The owner was right. The bull didn't look aggressive, as if he were going to charge, but he also didn't look as if he would move just because I asked him to. I decided that discretion was in order. Well, okay, I began to shake with fear. I climbed over the barbed wire fence. The bull watched me impassively, no expression on his face whatsoever. Except, I thought—and this might have been my imagination—I saw just a hint of amusement, just the flicker of a smile on his face as he watched me tear my blue jeans on a barb and gash my thumb on another. I was in a hurry and glancing at the ground because I was still very near the area of snake dens and didn't want to jump down on a rattler.

While I walked to my truck, the bull slowly turned and watched me. I had parked the truck with the driver's side door almost touching the gate. His head was now over the flimsy gate. I decided to get in on the passenger's side. Nope. Passenger side door locked. Keys inside truck. I sneaked around the truck. When I opened the door, I could have reached out and patted him on the head. I didn't. Instead, I jumped in the truck and roared off in a cloud of dust. It only took about ten minutes for my hands to stop shaking. Who would ever think that climbing to the highpoint of North Dakota, North Dakota of all states, would be so frightening?

I drove back to Amidon to buy a gift for the owner, maybe some flowers or candy. Both stores in Amidon were closed; it was Labor Day. I'll stick a five-dollar bill in an envelope and mail it to her. Her address was on the map. All I had was a twenty. Aw, what the heck. I stuck the twenty along with a thank-you note in the envelope and dropped it in a nearby mailbox. She could probably use it, and she was very nice.

As I headed for home across the exciting terrain of North Dakota, I began wondering about my adventure on White Butte. I was more frightened on this hike than on any of my other climbs, which at that time numbered about thirty. Some of those thirty climbs were up peaks that are among the highest in the lower forty-nine states. What disturbed me most was that what frightened me posed no real threat. Both the storeowner and the owner of White Butte had warned me about the rattlesnakes. They considered them a danger, so I, remembering my experience in snake country, walked through the area with caution, but not trepidation. But because of my single experience with a bull many years ago, this bull terrified me even though the owner had dismissed the animal as harmless if left alone. I had experienced the fear that Franklin Roosevelt referred to in his 1933 inaugural address when he said, "...the only thing we have to fear is fear itself—nameless, unreasoning, unjustified terror...." It can cause a nation or an individual to think and act irrationally. I wanted to say that I will never again allow myself to be terrified of something that I know is harmless or can be rendered harmless by intelligent action, but I knew I couldn't truthfully say that. Seldom can a person reason away irrational fear. That's why Roosevelt said that we need to fear it. I began to worry about our nation.

*Billie Louise Jones*
*Hot Springs, AR*

# These Days

"These days, you never know what will happen next," Jim Carpenter remarked to his wife, with a shake of his head to show that it was beyond words to tell.

He was commenting on a drama that burst out of the static on their CB. A wrecker driver had been fired on by the driver of a passing GMC pickup truck and struck in the leg. He did not know who was in the GMC. It came out of the night, fired at him, and went on by. The wrecker driver put out an emergency call on his CB.

It was one thirty in the morning, dark, cold, lonely on the highway. The headlights passed over pine trees bowed by the weight of ice and snow. They were driving from Waco, Texas, to spend Christmas with Lee Ann's parents in Shreveport, La. It had been record cold in East Texas that year; when they got to the piney woods, the roads turned icy and got worse as they went along. Carpenter concentrated his attention on the fourlane road ahead, careful but not worried about it. His car took the road steadily. He drove a ten year old Cadillac, long and black, because he believed they were better made than new cars.

Carpenter's face sharpened a little when he drove over an icy bridge, then returned to its natural set, a still face, alert eyes. A lean faced, lanky man in range clothes, he gave the impression of much weathering by sun and wind and outdoor work, though this was not the case. He had shaggy dark blond hair and a lighter mustache. He glanced at Lee Ann, dozing with her head on her arm, light brown hair falling over her face. A small, pale, pretty woman, she looked colorless and soft. The thought made him smile. She was wiry and obdurate. The rear view mirror showed the children, Jeff and Tosha, and Honey, the cocker spaniel, asleep in a pile together on the back seat. Five and eight, their hair was still yellow and their faces round. He thought of them that morning, strutting proudly to show off new shearling-lined suede jackets like their parents.' Lee Ann herded the family into the car, all of them alike in jackets and jeans, cowboy boots and hats; and Honey ran circles around them barking. His eyes crinkled up. Even with people around, he seldom showed much more sign of amusement and affection. He wanted to call back the memory with a word to Lee Ann.

She stretched herself awake. "Want me to drive awhile? You could put Jeff and Tosha in the front seat and get some rest back there."

He turned to her a little with what he was going to say taking shape in his mind when a pickup truck roared backwards out of a dark country road. Cursing, Carpenter swerved the Cadillac around the truck and went on down the highway.

After a moment he said, "Big Sandy is about ten-twelve miles ahead. Let's make a pit stop there."

He saw the pickup come up behind him and then turn into the other lane.

He supposed the driver meant to pass. The pickup pulled alongside him —close; coming too close, he thought— and rammed into the Cadillac. Carpenter was too shocked to think. That was only an instant. Then he knew: he's trying to force us off the road.

Lee Ann caught her breath with a sharp sound. "My God! The bastard wants to kill us!"

The children and dog were thrown down. The truck drew back and rammed again, and the children screamed and the dog howled. The truck kept ramming. Carpenter could not see the face of the driver. It was just pure malignancy bearing down on them out of nowhere. The road was dark; there was no one else on the road to see, to help. The car went into a spin. It went into the ditch. The children screamed and the dog howled, Lee Ann thudded against the door and clung to the seat, car crashed against car, the Cadillac rocked. But Carpenter wiped out everything except what he had to do now, keep the car from rolling over. The truck rammed it again and drove them further into the ditch, until they were wedged against the bank.

Carpenter could see the truck better now: a GMC pickup. The CB emergency call flashed trough his mind. He understood the worst possible that could happen.

He punched the button to lower the window and drew his Smith and Wesson automatic out of his shoulder holster. He fired six rounds at the grill of the GMC.

Under fire, it drew back and then went up the road gathering speed.

"He's gone!" Carpenter got another clip out of the glove compartment, holstered his gun, and rested his hands on the wheel. They were suddenly trembling.

"If this bank wasn't so steep," Lee Ann said shakily, "we would have rolled on over."

The children cried for her. She flipped her sinewy body over the seat. Carpenter heard her crooning to them.

He reached for the CB. "Breaker! Breaker! This here is the Waco Kid just out of Big Sandy. We were rammed and driven off the road by a GMC pickup. Believe it's the same one y'all heard about before. He's heading toward Big Sandy. Get smokey on his tail, you hear."

The CB crackled. "This here is the Leprechaun at Big Sandy Gas and Oil. We read you, Waco Kid."

"Let's see if this thing still runs," Carpenter said. The engine faltered, then caught. The Cadillac bucked and heaved itself at the road and fell back grunting into the ditch. Carpenter had trouble opening the car door. The cold was biting. He looked up and down the road warily. Then he got down in the ditch and pushed. With that and Lee Ann working the wheel, the car caught hold of the road and pulled back up. It was lucky the ground was frozen hard. If it had been soft, the Cadillac could not have gotten out of the ditch.

The car was barely rolling. "We'll stop at Big Sandy," he said. "Repairs. And we better put up for the night."

Lee Ann nodded agreement. Jeff and Tosha had stopped crying, though there was a sniffle now and then and Honey moved restlessly and growled. The children had their arms around each other, eyes big in white faces, frightened and not knowing and helpless. Carpenter thought if he told them nothing was wrong anymore, they would know this was not true and be even more afraid, even though they did not know what was happening.

Lee Ann reached out, and he dropped one hand to hold hers. Love wanted a touch to seal any moment of intense emotion —the GMC came over the hill driving head-on at them.

"Take the wheel!" Carpenter shouted and opened the door.

Lee Ann understood at once and did not hesitate.

Carpenter landed running and drew his gun. The GMC lights flared blindingly, but Carpenter looked just over them. He fired where the driver should be. The car lights hit the GMC just then. He saw the window shatter, the driver throw up his hand, a gun fly, blood. He did not see the driver's face because then the GMC turned out of the field of the car lights.

The GMC aimed itself where Carpenter was in the road. Carpenter saw that Lee Ann got the Cadillac around the GMC and kept going.

Carpenter never stopped moving, never became a still target. He fired again and thought he hit a tire. The GMC came on. He fired twice more at it. It bore down on him like nothing could stop it. He jumped off the road and ran toward it, firing. The GMC came closer and came alongside him and passed him, missing by inches.

Carpenter hit the dirt and rolled over into the ditch. It was dark there in the shadows of low-spreading young pines. He saw the GMC jerk to a halt. He steadied his gun elbow on the hard earth. For this one, only the driver and make it sure. The GMC rolled back, then rolled forward and lurched into a faster gear. It went over a low hill into the night.

Carpenter let go. His whole length went limp on the icy ground. Only for a moment; a sudden prickling up his spine warned that this might not be over yet. He had been sweating heavily. Now that turned cold on his skin. He reached inside his jacket for his red bandana and wiped his face. He got up, ready to spring back to cover instantly. His eyes and ears strained at the low hill and the blackness beyond. There was only the sound of the wind sweeping through the pines. Holding his Smith and Wesson and watching over his shoulder, he set off down the highway.

He saw the law coming, two cars. He stepped out on the road so their lights would hit him and waved. They drew over as if they were looking for him. The man in the lead car leaned over to open the passenger door for him. Carpenter saw a bulky man with a pouched face.

"Waco Kid? I'm J. D. Lovell, Police Chief of Big Sandy."

Carpenter tersely told him what had happened.

Lovell started the car and reached for his CB. "Breaker! Breaker! All you good buddies out there in the big rigs, this here is the Big Smokey. Police Chief J. D. Lovell of Big Sandy. We're chasing a maniac GMC. It's fired on two other vehicles. If there is a noninflammable rig approaching mile marker nineteen leading into Big Sandy, would you pull across the road and blockade this thing? Ten four."

Carpenter turned to Chief Lovell with a question, but the big man spoke at once. "Your wife's okay. She made it into the Big Sandy Gas and Oil Service Station. I was already on my way into town because the night attendant there had notified me of that wrecker driver's distress call. Then the boys —he jerked his head back to indicate the other car— and I got your call."

A clear sound came out of the CB static. "This here's the Cottonmouth pushing an eighteen wheeler up your way. Have I got the Big Smokey?"

"You got him, Cottonmouth. Go ahead."

"I've turned my rig out. Position just above the nineteen mile marker. And here he comes!"

Lovell hit the siren, and the two police cars really moved out. A few minutes later, the lights picked up the big rig straddling the highway and the GMC. The police cars squealed to a stop, and then men jumped out with drawn guns. The revolving red lights circled over the piney woods and the long, empty stretch of road, turning the familiar area into the grotesque terrain of nightmares. Carpenter saw the Cottonmouth's broad, bearded face in the cab window. The trucker seemed to have a gun resting on his door frame, but there was no sign of it when he climbed out of his rig.

There was no sound or movement from the GMC. There seemed to be a figure slumped over in the seat. The Chief and the two officers surrounded the GMC.

"You there! Come on out with your hands up."

Lovell ordered him out several times before the door opened and he slid out. He was bent over, so at first there was nothing Carpenter could see of him but frizzy blond hair. He raised his arms, but weaved back unsteadily. Carpenter saw blood on the man's sleeve where he had been shot. One officer grabbed him and pushed him against the GMC, and the other knelt to pat him down. His head fell back. The circling red lights moved over his face. It was a callow face, young but not a kid, deeply pitted with acne scars, openmouthed and blank.

Carpenter walked over to him and just looked at him. He thought, This man might have killed my whole family.

Lovell let him out at the Big Sandy Gas and Oil Service Station at the edge of the little town. The Police Chief said, "We'll run this boy in, and I'll come back for you. We'll need you at the arraignment. You go see your family now."

Lee Ann ran out of the service station, her arms wide. Carpenter held her close, kissing and touched to make himself sure she was safe. She reached up to pat his hair. Her eyes were streaming even while her mouth trembled up in a sort of smile.

"I can't stop crying. It's all over now and I can't stop crying. Isn't that funny?"

He walked her into the service station. Jeff and Tosha were petting the dog; it looked at first like play but it was really needing to hold onto something. Carpenter gathered them into his arms.

"Everything is all right now, kiddies," he said over and over.

Lee Ann wiped her eyes and got some coffee for him. Doing something useful helped her get herself together. The children settled down on a cot, their downy chick heads close together, though they did not go to sleep. Carpenter thought the bad trip was already fading out of their minds; but then at moments he thought he saw a stunned look cross their faces, an effect of horror remembered but too much for them to grasp. Honey growled in her sleep.

The night man at the service station, a slight, greying man, had a CV set up in the station to pass the night hours. He was the Leprechaun who had transmitted the messages to Lovell. He was solicitous of the family and did what he could for the Cadillac. He was friendly and curious, and he edged respectfully up to the subject of Carpenter's gun.

"Good idea, I guess," he said, "to have a gun on long night trips. Have you ever had much trouble before?"

"It's the first time I've actually had to use my gun. I hope I never do again. Once you know a little bit about some of the characters out there, you have to think about what you'll do if....You can't let them take over."

With that, the reaction hit him at last. His whole body shuddered. He drove his fist into his palm again and again.

J. D. Lovell, now that Carpenter could see him in clear light, was stout and red-faced, awkward-looking but probably strong. He had small, cold blue eyes and a very soft, courteous way; of speaking. "I took the boy in, but we'll have to arraign him later. He's too drunk to understand the charges against him. I'm sorry, but I'll have to ask you to stay. We'll need your statement."

"Of course. And I'll gladly come back for the trial." Then he burst out, "Who is he? What do you know about him? Why did he do this? Why!"

Lovell slowly shook his head and said regretfully, "Wish I could tell you, but I don't understand it myself. There's just no accounting for the things people can get up to. I will say that we found some tablets of what they call 'controlled substances' in the GMC. You did some good thinking through this whole thing." The Police Chief hesitated then said apologetically, "I really do hope you got a permit for that gun."

Carpenter pulled out his wallet and opened it to show his permit. "I'm a psychiatrist," he explained. "One of my patients threatened me and followed me, so I got the gun."

"I be damned. Well, Doc, you ought to be able to explain all this to me ."

Carpenter laughed dryly. "When I was in training, I had all the answers. Now I don't know anything. Some older colleagues report they're getting more cases of sociopathy now than they ever saw before. No one even knows what that statistic means. There hasn't been a big enough change in child rearing techniques to create a paradigm shift in personality. None of the theories of psychology seem big enough, deep enough to cover what is happening now. I can't explain anything. That's just the way it is, these days."

**Daniel D. Molinoff**
**Larchmont, New York**

## Passage

Greying on his linen cross
starved for flesh
dieting by metastase
deaf to morphine melodies
swelling in his veins,
gavels pound death away.

Shades of other fleeing souls
pass beyond without delay
still he stares, uncomprehending
for endless intravenous days
at fluorescent peaks
of distant Stygian shores
drifting off the screen.

Shrinking headlines hold him fast
Starched, pretending angels
softly closing open doors,
sorrows drying,
muted prayers for dignity
lost in the braying vanities
of medicine and law
that preserve him
as a living symbol *of* the dead.

Betrayed by time, by promises
of love (and life) long-lasting
he nods at me as I wait
with empty hypodermic oar
poised to push the plunger home,
his smile forgiving
when I finally choose
and ferry him out of reach.

**Barbara Smith**
**Philippi, WV**

## Character Analysis

Say what you will about clothes make the man or
You are what you customarily eat or
You can tell a fella by what's in his pockets.

My observation pertains to dogs
Like them as lies under the porches.
Of the beatinest up old flaky trailers,
Them dogs as mangy and likewise filth-ridden as
Their trash-tracking, four-lettered owners,
It seems to me that ever one *of* them mutts
Is a runaway, stray soul just out there looking
For some kind *of* something for over their heads and
Some kind *of* something for their ever-empty bellies,
Just like the creatures living up in the trailers
That they both has come to call home,

Or how about them soul-scary animals,
Them big beasts behind beware-of-dog fences
On chains that are fixing to let go and let loose
The next time some down-and-out dummy walks by
In which case that dummy ends up appetizer
For the next giant can *of* warmed-over horsemeat,

Or them dogs they showed *off* at the Boone County fair,
Them bounding balls *of* sheep-chasing beauty
Schooled to good. manners by gentleman farmers
With not another damned thing in this whole world to do
'Til them dogs knows chasing as their sole blessed business
On this or any other twirling planet,

Or them little Chiwawas with such god-awful tempers
That it makes a fella wonder they was ever created.

My point is this:
If you want to know what a man truly looks like
Or how he'll behave when the chips are thrown down,
Just check under' his porch or behind his quarters
Or just plain out ask for a few canine facts.
I got me no doubt and I am not lying.
You can tell a whole lot about any such person
By checking out the company he keeps.

*Lucy Smith*
*St. Paul, MN*

# Letters to Mr. S.

Dear Mr. S.,

When will I see my son? I am now out of the hospital and I have rented a small apartment.

Nothing fancy but it is clean and convenient for us. The rent is only 80 dollars- which is all I can afford on my 200dollars a month that you got for us in court. I also had to buy furniture because the apartment is unfurnished.

It is not really furniture but an assemblage of things: a chest of drawers for 25 dollars, a picnic table with two benches, which people are using outside in their backyards, but I am using it inside like they did in the Gothic castles and because I got the whole set for 20 dollars. Finally for 15 dollars I took a twin bed, which is narrow and single without its other twin brother-bed, just like a lonely me. I still have a baby-crib for my son which he can use a while longer before he outgrows it. Maybe then I will have work and more money to buy him a nice big bed and the shelves filled with toys.

But I am ready for him right now! The floor is waxed, there is a table cloth on our picnic table, and a Teddy-bear sits on the picnic bench. Please, let me know when I can see him. You are very kind to us though I know that as an attorney you must be very busy and have many more clients than me.

Forgive me if I write too much, but now, when I am no longer in the hospital where I got to know the nurses and other patients, the town is alien and empty for me. When I walk through the streets I see around me only the shadows with blank faces. Sometimes, when one of these shadows turns its blank face toward me as if looking at me, I realize that's because I have been talking to myself. Even the streets don't like me, I can't distinguish one from another, they're like a big spider web where I am caught like a helpless fly.

It all happened so soon after my arrival here —the breakdown of my marriage, my sickness, followed by a long hospital stay, and separation from my son —that I didn't have time to get to know anyone in this town. What would they want with me anyway, a stranger, a foreigner, without a country, without a family, rejected by her husband... I need to see my boy, to be with him. I hope that he still remembers me. That he knows who I am.

Well, I am really sorry for writing so much. I know how busy you are. I shouldn't importune you. Just let me know about my boy when you can. I miss him so much.

Dear Mr. S.,

I don't know what to do. They did bring my boy. He looks so much taller than when I saw him last time. Taller and thinner and he is afraid of me.

I can understand that. He didn't see me for several months which is a very long time at his age, but I think there is more to it than that. You see, he calls me now by my first name, but he calls my husband's mistress "mummy" when she speaks to him, and she uses my first name when she speaks about me. They came here several times since they left him with me , and each time, when they are leaving my apartment, she turns toward my son saying "don't worry darling, mummy will come really soon to see you, be brave"

It is as if I were a baby-sitter or worse, and my son looks at me with fear in his eyes. It breaks my heart. Do I have to accept this? I don't want to separate my son from his father, but when they are here, my husband hardly speaks to my boy, he just watches her speaking to him. I think that it is my husband who should relate to his son. Why does she need to come here?

Dear Mr. S.,

Thank you very much for getting the court order limiting visitation only to the father. It will help, I hope because we need some peace, some time to adjust again to each other without meddlers.

It has been difficult. I can't do anything right for my son. When I put the meal on the table or prepare a bath for him, or try to give him a medication for his cough, my little boy stiffens, clenches his teeth and his fists, looks at me coldly and says "I will tell my dad."

When he does that he isn't a four years old anymore, he is big, bigger than me, as big as his father and he is also rejecting me. He looks at me defiantly repeating his "I'll tell my dad."

I don't know what to do. I have to wash him from time to time ( he used to like it) so I try to undress him in spite of his postures, but he screams and I am afraid that all the neighbors will hear his screaming, denounce me to Welfare and I'll lose him.

I am afraid of Welfare. Recently, I got a letter from them questioning the number of colds my son has. Apparently my husband complained and now, even if I make sure that he is dressed warm when we go out, it seems that every cold he has is caused by me. Though Dr. Spock says that every child under six is prone to many colds, those other kids have two parents and no one pays attention to them. But with me it is different. I don't know anyone here, but everyone seems to watch me. I can't be me. I can't relate to my son under all those watchful eyes. I can't be direct with him.

I am afraid. I don't know whom to trust. I+ will not send you this letter because I am afraid even of you. Well, I am not afraid of you but I don't know if you would have to report it if I tell you this, and the people from Welfare would consider me a bad mother and take my son from me, and who will defend me? Even my son could say so and would call for his dad. Yesterday I was so upset when he said that again, that I opened the door and I told my little boy " go out, go and tell your dad." He looked at me frightened. But really it is me who is increasingly afraid.

I have reason to be afraid. I am a nobody and everybody can judge me.

When I was in the hospital, a young woman came one day to see me, asked me few insignificant questions and left. I learned later that she wrote a report about my housekeeping because she was sent to investigate my competency as a mother or housekeeper- apparently this considers to be the same. She was investigating for the court, and she reported that I was a poor housekeeper. I don't know how she knew that because at that time I didn't have a house to keep. I was in the hospital and the bed I was in, belonged to the hospital and was cared for by the hospital as well as everything else in that room, its windows, its floor. So how could she know anything about me? That's why I am afraid because everybody can say anything and be believed, and who would believe me?

Dear Mr. S.,

I don't know if I will send you this letter either, but I must write it. I'll decide later if I send it or not.

I am grateful for several months of peace I got because of the court order keeping my husband's mistress away. They didn't come to see us since that order, though I think it would be good if my son could see his dad. All the same, things began to be better. My son is going to a nursery, I started to study, and I have a part time job. Just few hours, but it helps. The nursery is also a great help, and the people there are nice not only to my son, but to me as well.

Every day, late afternoon, I bring him home from the nursery and we have a quiet time together. We often watch T.V. which someone gave us. We watch "Mr. Rogers" or "Sesame Street" recommended by his nursery teacher. It really is good and helps both of us in our English. My son speaks now quite well.

He was late in learning to talk because when we came here he was just ready to start to speak, and I couldn't help him because I didn't know in which language I should speak to him. My husband, being from here, wanted him to learn English, but he was at work all day, and I didn't know English that well. I knew Polish, my mother tongue, well, but it would be useless here to my son. There was also French, language which I used with my husband before we came here, and I always hoped that my son would learn it. If my son could hear us communicating in French as we used to do, he would learn it so fast and easily. He would just imitate us, and he would learn because he would want to be just like us. He would want to do everything that we would do, and he would eat everything that we ate, because it would be important for him to be like us.

But there is no "us" here. There's no one but me and my son doesn't want to be like me. He likes his nursery, people there are like everybody else, while I am not. When I pick him up at the nursery and ask how his day was, or I speak to his teachers, other children talk about me to my son, they say " your mom speaks funny"

He doesn't want to learn anything from me. When he says "fum" instead of thumb and I try to correct him, he looks at me and says again "fum." I think that he is afraid that if he repeats after me he'll be talking funny too.

At home when we sit down to dinner, the only meal of the day we have together because he has breakfast and lunch in nursery, he looks suspiciously at the food: "what's that" -he says-"we don't eat thaaat in the nursery" People always talk about "mother's cooking." There are many restaurants with names like "Mama's Kitchen." I had hoped that some day my son would remember my food, that we would share the taste of dishes from my country, from my childhood, but how could he remember my cooking when he rejects it?

It is a great help to me, the nursery, but it is again like another home for my son and somehow this other home is right and mine is wrong. I know that it isn't just the nursery but a division between the mother's house and father's house. He learned there that my house and me are no good, and that everything else is better. Maybe it is true, for what can I give him except my love?

Dear Mr. S.,
My husband is not my husband anymore. I know it and I don't know it. It is so strange. It took a whole year before it happened and then it happened so fast.

There was a judge (I remember only his black robe, not him) and me, and you. My husband wasn't there. I don't know what has been said, I was too confused. It was even printed in a daily newspaper under "Divorces," why would anyone be interested in that?

I wouldn't know about this being in the newspaper if someone didn't bring it to me the day it was printed. The man who brought the newspaper had started few times my old car during the last winter. He works in a nearby garage and has never visited me before. He came with another man whom I didn't know and tried to offer me some work. It was really nice of him, he asked if I do a blow job, but I didn't know what it could be and asked him what it was. He didn't tell me. He just looked at the other man and said "let's go" and they left. I still wonder what it could be?

I put away the newspaper for a keepsake. I don't know why.

Dear Mr. S.,
You say that my husband is married? Two weeks after divorce? That he filed another petition to the court for the right of seeing his son? I never prevented him from seeing his son. He himself wasn't coming here anymore!

I wrote this to the judge. I am sending this to you to look at. Is it O.K.? Can I show it to him?

Dear Judge,
You have said that you care for the best interest of the child and I agree with you. I think that my son, that any child, should see both of his parents, but I think that a child isn't a parcel to be shipped back and forth from parent to parent because when it happens, the child lives in the mother's house or in the father's house, but where is the child's house?

Dear Mr. S.,

I don't understand. I didn't say anything in the court you didn't want me to say, and I didn't use my letter because you said it would be wrong to do it. So why did the judge say that now it is O.K. for my husband to bring my son to his new wife because they are married? This is the same judge who said before that she shouldn't see my son. I thought that it was because she was turning my son against me! I thought that he really meant what he said about the best interest of the child. Why it is different now? Because they have marriage certificate? What difference does it make to a five years old?

I am not writing this to Mr. S. I am writing this to myself as I saw it. I need to talk. I can't talk.

There was a knock at the door. A cold-polite look on my husband's face. A confused look on my son's face. In the dark below, the car door was opened. In the dim light from inside of the car appeared the head of the other woman and turned toward my husband and my son who were emerging from the darkness and joining her in the car. When the door closed they all disappeared, only the headlights still illuminated the road for a few seconds, while the car was moving toward darkness.

There was nothing left to be seen below. There was nothing to look at around me in my apartment. There was an immense emptiness within me, and I was suddenly very tired . I was a hundred years old and ready for eternal rest. So I undressed and lay down alone in my twin bed which seemed too big for me.

Dear Mr. S.,
Everyone here says that boys raised by a mother need a "father figure," that's how it is called. They say that's especially important for my son, because I am a foreigner and his father doesn't come to see him. His father didn't come since his new wife had a child, also a boy, two years ago. At first I thought that it was good because we could be together and learn to trust each other. Now I think that maybe the people who say that he needs a man, are right. Teachers say that he is very shy at school. He isn't shy at home. I noticed that I can't talk to any man in his presence because he is disruptive and interrupts all conversations. It is as if he felt that every man should belong to him and not to me. I think that he could be satisfied with just one man, but his father is not coming. How can I find him such a man?

Dear Mr. S.,

Thank you for telling me about the "Big Brothers." The Big Brother that my son got is married.

He and his wife are very nice people and they take my son with them every Sunday afternoon. They play cards with him and teach him a lot of funny songs which all children here know, but which I couldn't teach him because I only know the children songs from my country. I should be very happy. I am happy for him. But when they take him out, I feel the same way as I felt when his father used to take him to his house. Why does he always have to be in two houses?

I wonder if it is good or bad?

Sometimes I think that I too was living in many houses. My country was the one house, this country is another house and there were some other houses-countries in between. But this was different because I lived in each country-home at a distinct time: one after another. First my old country, then other countries, and finally this new country.

My son seems to live in many different houses at the same time and he is torn in different directions. He can't sit still anymore because of that. He is so restless that he can't concentrate and he has very hard time learning at school. I don't know what to do about it.

Dear Mr. S.,

I am sorry to bother you, we were in court so many times because of this, but again I didn't get child support. The type of work I can get pays very little, with no benefits at all. I had to drop my studies when my son went to school because I had no one to leave him with when he was returning from school. Even when I was getting child support it wasn't enough to pay a baby-sitter, especially when I can't afford to buy many needed things.

It is also so hard to say"no" to so many things my son asks for. It is too much for me to go out with him for a walk through the streets full of stores where everything is a temptation. I don't know what to tell him in the food store bursting with delicacies, when I have to take only the few cheapest items. Even at home, when we try to relax watching T.V. there are advertisements pushing all kind of things and toys, which he says right away that he wants. I tried to watch only public T.V. but he learned about the shows on other channels and wanted to watch them. I couldn't stop him just because of advertisements, but it is hard to say "no" and "no" all the time to so many things.

It makes me look like a bad mother who doesn't want to give him anything, though I am the only one who gives him everything that he has, and all that I can I give. I have no help because his father sends only ten or fifteen dollars once or twice after each appearance in the court and then stops sending anything again. I don't know if you can help me. I don't know if anyone can.

Dear Mr. S..

It has been many years since I last wrote you. I am writing now because I think that I saw a glimpse of you in a passing car, yesterday. Maybe it wasn't you but it make me think about you and how important you used to be for us, how many times you helped us out of trouble.

Maybe you would like to know what became of us? Somehow we made it. I don't know how. My son kept growing and he is grown up.

Though he moved out, he calls me sometimes and visits occassionally. I look at this young man, whom I know so slightly and yet so deeply, with strong emotions, because he carries within him so much of my life and more of me that even if he knew he would never admit.

We have made it, though I don't know what that means. I think we made it through, but we still carry so much pain. It bonds us as well as divides us and I still wonder why we had to have it so hard?

M. Lewis Stein
Irvine, CA

# Homecoming

Ellis Coffman stepped off the 12-seater plane into an icy wind. He remembered such winds from his youth in this small Upper Michigan town but the blast of air was still shocking in its suddenness, lashing his face and piercing his fur-lined raincoat. A woman emerged from the squat brick building that served as the airport's terminal, and they embraced. At 38, his sister, Edith, was six years younger than he but, in the cold, her pinched face and haggard eyes made her look older.In the late November evening, Ellis could see traces of snow that, in another month or less, would smother the region. He stamped his feet to restore circulation to his legs and rubbed his bearded face to offset its rapid chilling.

"How is she"? he asked.

"She's dying," Edith replied. "Anyway, she says she's dying and that if we don't take her out of the nursing home she'll die tomorrow."

Ellis was coming from one death to another. His wife, Marilyn,whom he loved, had died of ovarian cancer two months earlier. Now, his mother, Lillian, the stocky, assertive businesswoman who had helped their late father build a thriving furniture store, had only days or weeks to live, according to her doctor.

"She hates the place and wants to go home," Edith continued. "I'd like to bring her home but she would need 24-hour care and we can't find anybody here who can give it."

Lillian was 84. Eight months earlier, she had broken her hip and then developed heart disease. Doctors at St. Anthony's Hospital in town said there was nothing more they could do for her and recommended the Anderson Nursing Home, the only such facility in Wolf Lake.

"How bad is the place"? Ellis inquired.

"Actually, it's not bad at all," Edith said. "It was built only five years ago and, for Wolf Lake, it's as good as we can expect. They keep it clean and the food is well prepared. There's a dietician there plus three nurses. Remember the old Pleasant Garden nursing dump on l5th Street. This one is miles better.But ma bitches about everything and she can't stand most of the other women there. And, Ellis, she forgets a lot of things, sometimes things that were said to her five minutes ago."

They got into Edith's Buick and she drove in silence to the Timberline Hotel, where Ellis had a reservation. Edith and his brother Leo, who ran the furniture store, had invited him to stay with them but Ellis declined. He dreaded conversations with Edith's husband, Harvey, an optometrist, who insisted on inflicting his left-of-center politics on Ellis, challenging him, as a political science professor, to embrace his various liberal causes. "I teach and write about political science, Harvey, I don't advocate causes or man the barricades," he once told him. Another time, out of Edith's earshot, he declared to his brother-in-law: "Honestly, I don't give a good goddamn about the Amazon rain forest, revision of the marijuana laws, or the rate of executions in Texas."

Nor would he spend three or four days at the home of Leo and his wife, Ro-

---

berta, a beauteous, dark-haired transplant from a wealthy Chicago suburb, who never missed an opportunity to invidiously compare it to Wolf Lake desite the pleading of her husband that her attitude was hurting his business. There was sure to be at least one argument between them during his stay.

Besides, Ellis had brought papers to grade and a first draft of a journal article to rework, labors he would find difficult to accomplish in either household. The hotel also seemed a better place to deal with his overwhelming grief over Marilyn's death and the continued estrangment of their only child, Judith, who had refused to return from her home in Florence for her mother's funeral.

It was too late to go to the nursing home and Edith left Ellis at the hotel with the notice that she would pick him up at ten in the morning for their visit to their mother.

"They don't like us to come earlier because they're giving them their medicines and bathing them," Edith said. Then, she made him promise that he would come to her house for dinner the following night.

Ellis was unpacking in his room when Leo phoned."I'm sorry I wasn't at the airport but I've got a kind of crisis here," his brother said. "A whole fucking truckload of stuff from Ethan Allen is missing someplace between here and Milwaukee—probably highjacked. How are things in California? Oh Christ, forget that question. It must be terrible for you with Marilyn gone."

Leo, three years older than Ellis, had been a star fullback in high school and earned a respectable record as a second-stringer at Michian State. At six feet, three and 230 pounds, he could still easily shove heavy furniture around the showroom.

"I'm all right," Ellis said. "Other than the highjacked truck, how are things going with you"?

"Oh, you know, Ellis, it's the slack season for us. When you have a chance come over and I'll go over the books with you." Ellis and Edith, who worked part-time as a billing clerk and typist in her husband's office, owned shares in the business, which provided them with an irregular income that depended on what kind of a year the store had.

He begged off Leo's offer to take him to dinner at the Northwoods Steakhouse, saying he was too tired.

But instead of going to bed, Ellis went down to the Wolf's Head bar in the hotel's basement. It had been a favorite watering place for him and his friends when he was home from college.The bar and its walls were constructed of split logs waxed to a shiny finish. The bartender was a plump blonde woman about 35, who was kidding around with three men, who were inviting her to go deer hunting with them. One pointed to a deer head on the wall, saying, "If you let me teach you to shoot, Charlene, you'll get a buck bigger than that one."

Charlene laughed. "What's your wife going to say when you and me are in the woods together"?

Before the man could reply, she noticed Ellis at the bar and came over, smiling."Hi, there" she said. "What can I get you"? He ordered a beer and a barbecued beef sandwich before lighting his second cigarette of the day as he looked around the room. He immediately spotted a high school pal, Mel Berquist, sitting with his wife, Lorraine, at a table near the small bandstand. Mel saw Ellis at the same time and strode toward the bar, his arm outstretched.

"For Christ's sake, Ellis, I didn't know you were in town," Mel exclaimed as they shook hands."How the hell are you? C'mon, join us." Mel, one of Wolf Lake's many blond Vikings, was a local lawyer. He and Lorraine, a pretty woman with short brown hair, were high school sweethearts, separated only when he went off to Northwestern and she to Michigan. She hugged Ellis and kissed him on the cheek as Charlene brought over his beer and sandwich. The Berquists were drinking brandy.

"What brings you back"? Mel asked.

Ellis told them about his mother. "Oh yeah,' Mel said. "I heard she was ill but I didn't know she was at Anderson."Is it bad?"

"She tells Edith she's dying. I'll see her tomorrow."

"This whole town is dying," Mel said. "Did you notice how dead downtown is? There are more empty store fronts every month. The mall near the fairgrounds is grabbing all the customers but it isn't doing so great either. We're thinking of getting out, too, but I don't know where the hell we would go."

Lorraine, who was a little drunk, said, "We're not going anywhere, Mel." You got a practice here for better or worse."

"If my practice gets any worse," we'd better start talking to a real estate agent," Mel persisted, smiling bleakly.

Ellis was not pleased with the conversation. He finished his sandwich and remained for a few more minutes before excusing himself, pleading a long day.

"I'll call you for drinks at the house," Mel called out as Ellis headed for the stairs. "Or maybe lunch at Rotary." Ellis gave a backward wave in retreat.

When Edith picked him up the next morning. Dark clouds hung over the town and a sharp wind was blowing specks of snow that he knew warned of a storm. The nursing home was on the edge of town on a small rise next to a pine forest. To Ellis, the well-landscaped,L-shaped building resembled one of the neat structures in the industrial park near his Santa Barbara home.

Inside, Edith led him to a sprawling recreation room containing about 15 women and three men. Some of the women were in wheelchairs. One clawed at the side of her chair while singing "Jingle Bells" in a cracked voice. Two patients playing cards told her to stop. When she wouldn't, they slammed down their cards and walked off.

Ellis and Edith found their mother in a wheelchair by a window, gazing at a calendar on the wall.

"I didn't think you'd be in time," said Lillian as she looked up at the two. When Ellis last saw her at the hospital six months ago, she had lost only a little weight and was cracking jokes about Leo being unable to run the store without her. Now, she was shriveled and shaking. When Ellis bent down to kiss her, she pushed him away.

"Not today, dear son," she said. "I smell bad. But you're a good boy to come here for my funeral."

"I didn't come for your funeral, Ellis lied.

"But that's what you'll get," Lillian whispered. "Did Edith tell you how much I despise this place and everybody in it? I want to go home to die." She began crying.

"I know," Ellis said, placing his hand on her bone-thin shoulder.He recalled the times when his mother, bristling with energy, would get them off to school in the morning and then drive to the furniture store for nearly a full day's work.

When Edith went to talk to one of the nurses, Lillian asked him about his life in California, a subject she always brought up during his homecomings. "And how is Marilyn"?

"Marilyn died, mother," Ellis said. "I wrote you."

Lillian nodded. "Oh yes.I forget things. I'm sorry. She was a kind person. I always liked her. You made a good marriage."

They were sitting at a small table scattered with worn pieces of a picture puzzle.The box displayed a drawing of a small white cottage near a pond dappled by a late afternoon sun piercing the trees. A boy about 10 years old stood by the pond holding a fishing pole made from a branch. As Ellis pushed one of the pieces with his finger, he noticed that four old women a few feet away were attentively listening to their conversation. He hated them immediately. Edith returned as Ellis stood up, rage boiling inside him. "Is there anywhere in this fucking place where we can have a little privacy"? he asked, keeping is voice low

"We can go to her room but she finds it even worse than here. That's the way it is here," Edith said.

Ellis swung around and stared directly at the women. They stared back but did not move. He and Edith stayed for another half hour until a nurse came out and said it was time for Lillian's lunch and medicine. As they drove away from the building, snow was falling heavily from a somber sky.

Plans were changed that night. Instead of dinner at Edith's house, Ellis dined at the home of Leo and Roberta. Edith and Harvey also were there. The discussion about Lillian began with drinks and continued through dinner.

"Let's bring her home," Ellis suggested, referring to the condominium she bought after the death of their father. For years, the family had lived in a huge frame house with an encircling porch and a lake view in the best part of town, now much too big for their mother alone.

"And who will take care of her day and night"? asked Edith. Her thin lips tightened as she looked steadily at Ellis. "As I told you before, we can't find any-one here to do that. There are only two private RNs in town and both are already loaded with patients."

Ellis drained the last of his wine. "Maybe," he ventured, although knowing what was coming, "she could stay with one of you.It won't be for long. You could try to get someone from Iron Ridge to come in at least part time? She would only have about a fifteen-minute drive."

"And what about the rest of the time"? Leo retorted. "She has ongoing medical needs. From where you sit in Santa Barbara, this situation may have easy answers, but we have to live with it right here. Edith did have ma in the house for three weeks and it was pure hell. She has to have constant attention."

"Even Dr.Gresky said she should be in a nursing home," Edith added, her face flushed. "Do you think we don't care about her"?

"Edith has done a lot for your mother that you don't know about," Harvey chimed in. Ellis thought about hurling a drink in his face but held back for his sister's sake.

"Okay, okay." "Forget that I mentioned it."

Leo put his arm around Ellis. "Jesus, Ellis," he said "you've got to under-stand that it's been a tough time for us. We only want what's best for her."

Roberta, smoking her third cigarette, stayed out of it. She  always had welcomed Ellis' return to Wolf Lake in the belief that he added some class to the family. At one point, he saw her wink at him while Leo and Edith were taking him on.

The evening ended cordially as Ellis and Leo reminisced about high school classmates and the time George Manley, the principal, threatened to disqualify half the football team for poor grades just before the big game with Rock River. They also joked about a  long-ago family trip to visit relatives in Milwaukee, who forgot to meet them at the train station.

Even so, Ellis had another near sleepless night after sitting for more than hour in the hotel bar, chatting with Charlene about her longing to see California some day and her husband who was in a Wisconsin prison for sticking up a pizza joint. When he finally dozed off, he dreamt of seeing his mother fleeing the nursing home in her nightgown while cursing her family.

Lillian died two days later. "Her heart gave out," Dr. Gresky told Leo by phone. While Edith made funeral arrangements in town, Leo and Ellis went to the nursing home to collect their mother's belongings, which included a few items of clothing and her jewelry. After dropping them in a bag and stuffing them in the trunk of the car, Leo remembered that the final bill for Lillian's care had to be settled. Ellis returned to the building with him because it was cold in the car. Inside, Leo headed for the office, leaving Ellis in the main room, where he studied activities notices on the bulletin board. A bus trip to a local Bingo parlor was scheduled for that night. He recalled that Lillian had ridiculed the home's Bingo players.

A thin, bright-eyed woman with  tufts of grey hair and wearing a pink flannel bathrobe over a nightgown steered her wheelchair to within a foot of him. Ellis turned as she touched his elbow.

"Could you take me to my room"? she asked.

"Of course," he replied. "Point the way"

The way was through a long corridor that split out from the big room. Ellis pushed her almost to the end of the hall before she ordered him to stop.

"Please wait," she said. The woman wheeled herself into her room and returned with a blue woolen shawl draped over her shoulders.

"Okay," she said, "let's go."

"What"?

"Out the door, right in front of you," she snapped, pointing to the exit consisting of two large doors with steel push-bars. "I want to go home."

"Where do you live"? A strange feeling came over him. Why the hell not, he thought.

"606 North Latham."

The address was five or six blocks away. Ellis knew how to get there. He turned the wheelchair around and backed out,using his body to shove open one of the heavy doors.

They emerged shortly before l o'clock into hazy sunshine that cut a little of the morning frigidity. It had stopped snowing. But even with his coat, Ellis was chilled. He wished he had brought gloves.

"How are you doing"? he asked the woman. "Are you warm enough"?

"I'm  Doris Beckstrom," she responded, ignoring his question. "Who are you"?

"My name is Ellis Coffman. Lillian Coffman was my mother. She lived at

Anderson. Did you know her"?

"Who?"

"Lillian Coffman. She died last night."

I don't know anybody there and they don't know me. They can all go to hell."

606 North Latham Street was a one-story frame house with a small concrete porch. Its white paint had turned grey in patches. There were no curtains in the front windows, one of which was cracked. Ellis mounted the five steps to the porch and knocked on the door. He waited a few seconds before knocking again, a process he repeated several times. Finally,by leaning over the porch rail, he was able to peer into the living room. It was bare of furniture.

"I don't believe anyone is here," Ellis told Doris, who sat huddled at the foot of the steps, her face stony.

"Well, I guess my husband is out some place," she said. "Tell you what. Let's go over to my sister Edna's house. It's over on the next block—Sixth Street." She began coughing, her breath white in the frigid air.

Ellis took off his coat and spread it over her lap before resuming their journey. They were turning into Sixth Street when Leo drove up beside them in his Lexus, slamming his brakes until they screeched. He jumped out and planted himself in front of the wheelchair, a hulking figure, his face twisted into rage and disbelief.

"What the fuck is the matter with you"? he yelled. "Have you gone crazy"?

"She said she wanted to go home, and I thought I would help her. Ellis remained calm.

"Home? She has no home. She's one of the major nut cases at Anderson's. You can get us all into a shit-pile of trouble for this."

"Well, I was taking her over to her sister's house."

"She has no sister, no family here. They're all dead,"Leo shouted. "She's ninety-five or ninety-six years old." He lifted Doris, a protesting, tiny bundle, out of the wheelchair  ordered Ellis to open the back door of his car and dropped her in. He then folded the wheelchair and jammed it in the trunk on top of Lillian's things.

"Maybe we can get back without the staff knowing about it," Leo said as they drove away, "Amy Hatcher, one of the patients, saw you two going out but she promised to keep quiet about it if I found you."

Doris began sobbing. "Why didn't you take me home"? she wailed.

At the nursing home, Leo's hope of secrecy had been wiped away. Marcia Morelock the supervising nurse, was at the door, he face grim, as Leo carried Doris to her room. After she was put to bed and  her temperature taken, Leo told Ellis to wait while he went into Mrs. Morelock's office.

He came out twenty minutes later, grabbed  Ellis by the arm, hustling him outside. In the car, Leo seemed relieved. "I got you off the hook unless she dies of pneumonia," he said. "But that was a goddamn stupid thing to do."

"Did she once live at 606 Latham"? Ellis inquired.

"Yeah, I guess so. Anyway, she's from Wolf Lake."

"How did you get me off the hook, Leo"?

Grinning, Leo turned to Ellis. "I told Marcia that grief over ma's death had made you kind of crazy for a little while, which is pretty close to the truth."

"That isn't true. I knew what I was doing."

"Who gives a fuck if it's true or not? The main thing is that Marcia's not going to report a kidnapping or something like that."

Neither Ellis nor Leo said anything more as they rode to Edith's house, where she had prepared lunch. As the three nibbled on sliced turkey sandwiches and salad, Leo told his sister what happened.

"I simply wanted to help her get home" Ellis explained.

Edith put her sandwich down. Her face was taut with anger. "You wanted to help her in a way we didn't help ma, is that it"? she demanded. "Dear, kind Ellis making amends for what his family failed to do. The old lady was mother, right"? You asshole, this will be all over town by tonight."

"It wasn't that way at all, but are you feeling guilty over anything"? Ellis said, his own anger rising.

Trembling, Edith rose, slapped his face and strode from the room. Ellis expected Leo to slug him but his brother only looked bemused.

"You've been gone a long time,Ellis," Leo noted."Like I said before, you don't know what it's been like here. But I think Edith was pretty goddamn close to the truth. She's taken most of the responsibility for ma in the past year and you dug it into her."

Ellis left the house for the hotel, where he packed for the trip home, deciding to skip the funeral. He told no one of his departure. He would apologize later.

The regional airline took him to Chicago, where he caught a United flight for Los Angeles. He sat in first class and slowly sipped the glass of Champagne placed on his tray before takeoff. Then he ordered another.

The wine helped him to deal honestly with Edith's accusation. A clear case of disconnect, he reasoned. He wondered how Doris was getting along. He planned to drop her a note.

*William Beyer*
*Belvidere, IL*

# A Father's Death; In Retrospect

Missing for six days,
your body was found
by two boys,
covered with snow,
in an area of dense woods;
far from home.

Your funeral
was brief,
unopened casket,
short eulogy,
your favorite hymn;
a final prayer.

We never knew what happened
in the woods,
exactly how you died;
why you were walking
miles from home
in mid Winter

After the funeral,
entering your small room,
I discover
that on a round brown table
you left a jigsaw puzzle
of a beach in Tahiti
half finished,
large Hershey bar
unopened,
and a gold pocket watch
still ticking.

**Anne Fauvell**
**Rapid City, SD**

## Rosemary, Sesame, and Caraway

Were
three daughters
in one family.
Folks said they came
from good seed.
Their father,
a medical doctor,
used herbs often.
He chewed spearmint
gum for his breath,
and just loved
mint jelly with
fig leaves,
Greek style.
Their mother, Sweet Allyssium,
wiped bee balm
on her upper lip.
She claimed
bee balm
sniffed, quieted
her nerves.
But in truth,
Mother enjoyed
a glass of white wine
with a hint
of a mint leaf
or two.
The brother,
Basil,
almost choked
on a cherry or two.
Yes! Life was quite
a neat snifter
for the Potting family.

* * *

## Hot Lipstick

In my purse,
in 105 degree weather,
proves too much.
A meltdown begins
with the hot lipstick
and me.
We are wilted,
hung over
when we enter the cool
house.
I place the red, hot lipstick
in the refrigerator.
I am reminded
when I was
a young woman,
living in a hot city
tenament apartment,
I placed my lipstick
in the ice box
to become cool
and firm with ice.
The lipstick did
just that
after many hours.
So here we are again.
Not with the same lipstick,
or the same color,
but the same method.
It is cool
to have a hot lipstick.
I hope even now
the lipstick
will remain hot
for a tender kiss,
or many kisses,
or for love.
How cool that would be.
At eighty, to have
hot lipstick.

\* \* \*

## He Weeps

How often, he weeps, indeed.
I saw him do that at least

six times
out of the twenty times
I saw him.
No matter!
Now he is ready to marry
again,
hump and bump a new woman.
Well, maybe
she will outlive him
this time.
It would just serve him
right.


\* \* \*


*William Arthur*
*Hopkins, Minnesota*

# Missing Branches

It was the perfect climbing tree: a silver maple in Robbinsdale that towered eighty feet tall in the Wilsons' back yard, plainly visible from our kitchen window. The sturdy branches started about five feet off the ground and wound in an upward spiral until the smallest ones were obscured behind the big green maple leaves.

Of course "Tony" knew all about this special tree. We didn't know his real name, but my wife called him Tony because that was her favorite name for a boy. Tony was the best tree-climber in the neighborhood and it was an annual rite of spring for Mary and I to watch him running over to try the tree for the first time. Standing near its base, Tony would jump and catch the first branch with both hands. Then he would "walk" his legs up the trunk until he could get one of them around a branch to pull himself up. A regular monkey, that Tony. In no time at all, he would disappear behind a maple leaf high in the tree.

Mary was afraid that he would fall the first time she saw him go up. "What if he should slip?" she asked me.

"You don't have to worry about that kid," I told her. "He's climbed trees before. Besides that, there's nothing we can do. It's the Wilsons' problem, not ours. If they don't want him climbing their tree, they'll say something."

I never did find out exactly what the Wilsons thought of Tony's tree-climbing. If they cared a great deal, they kept it a secret. Of course the Wilsons weren't home very often. Maybe they didn't know about Tony. In any case, Mary took to being Tony's protector. Every time she saw him run over to climb the tree, she would drop whatever she was doing and watch at the kitchen window until he came safely down.

The next spring Mary got pregnant. I was sitting in the living room one afternoon reading the paper by the sunlight when I heard her say dreamily, "that's the kind of son I want us to have...."

"What...?" I looked up and saw she was staring out the window at the Wilsons' silver maple.

"Like Tony," she said. "He seems like such a nice boy. That's the kind of son I want us to have."

The paper dropped from my hands unnoticed as I got up and walked toward her. I held Mary close and kissed her very tenderly. "Don't worry, darling," I whispered. "We will. By this time next year, you'll have your very own son."

The days followed in quick succession during Mary's pregnancy. She had never been happier. It was her first baby and we had both wanted one for so long. Of course there were minor complications. The baby seemed to be growing a little large and Mary was a small woman. But the doctors said not to worry. Nature would take its course.

By November Mary's profile gave her the appearance of an overripe watermelon bursting with juice and ready to be harvested. On the eighth her labor pains started. She was quiet and resigned during the drive to the hospital, but once there she clung desperately to me and wouldn't let go. "Don't leave me," she begged. "Please don't leave me!"

How could I tell her that a film I saw on childbirth had made me violently ill? "Don't worry," I consoled her. "You'll be all right."

A nurse came and took her away, but not before I saw Mary burst suddenly into tears.

In the waiting room I reasoned that Mary's display of emotions was typical of a woman about to become a mother. As time went by, though, I began to worry that I should have stayed with her.

After three hours a doctor came out. "Sorry to keep you waiting so long," he said, "but the baby's head is turned the wrong way. We're going to have to perform a Caesarean section on your wife."

"Is that serious?" I asked.

"Just a routine operation," he assured me.

Despite the doctor's words, I was seized by a strange sense of foreboding. Why didn't I have the stomach to be with my wife when she needed me most? Trying to purge my guilt and fears, I prayed desperately on my knees. "Please God, don't let anything happen to my baby. Don't let anything happen to Mary!"

The praying calmed my nerves and I fell into a fitful sleep. At 8 a.m. a nurse woke me. Both Mary and her ten-pound baby boy were dead. Something about toxemia. I didn't care about the medical terms. The only thing that mattered was that I had never felt so alone.

It was a hard winter, a gray winter, a cold winter, a snowy winter. In February I traveled to Acapulco, trying to forget. The first day on the beach I took a look at the sun-drenched revelers around me and felt worse than ever. Every woman reminded me of Mary. Every little boy reminded me of my dead son. After three days I returned to Robbinsdale.

I got through the nights with Sominex and double-bourbon chasers. Even then I would sometimes wake restlessly at 3 a.m. to think of Mary. Wishing that she hadn't gotten pregnant. Wishing that she hadn't died. Wishing....

But no, I wasn't that crazy. At least not yet. There was a time for every living thing to die. My time would come soon enough.

And then, relentlessly it seemed to me, the weather warmed up and it was spring again. The sun streaming through the windows as I watched television only depressed me more. It was on just this kind of day that I had promised Mary a boy like Tony. I got up and went to the refrigerator for another Pabst. Just the thing to dull my mind for a little longer and keep me from thinking too much.

On the way back I saw Tony, running as fast as he could toward his favorite tree. It was the annual rite of spring. Only I knew something about that tree that Tony didn't know yet. A man from the nursery had come to the Wilsons' house two days before. He had pruned the bottom two branches of the tree and covered the stubs with tree paint to keep the sap from running. The lowest branch on the perfect climbing tree now started at ten feet. Maybe the Wilsons didn't want Tony to climb their tree after all.

I walked to the kitchen and stood at the window to see how Tony would fare. He reached the tree and stopped short when he saw the branch stubs; but I knew he would try to climb the tree, missing branches or not. Two or three leaps for the lowest branch with his arms outstretched fell far short. Then Tony tried to shinny up the trunk like a small bear cub. The tree's great girth prevented him from getting a good grip, though. He slid down as much as he went up. As a last resort, Tony found part of one missing branch that had been left behind by the nursery. By leaning this log-sized piece up against the trunk and standing on it, he was able to grasp the lowest branch of the tree. But the branch was too thick for Tony to get a good grip and his hands kept slipping off. Twice he fell heavily to the ground only to pick himself up and try again. When I saw him fall the third time, I knew it was hopeless. Tony's annual rite of spring had come to an end.

Turning away, I finished the beer and then looked in the refrigerator for another. But there were no more. All I had left of the four six-packs of beer that I had bought two days ago were twenty-four empty cans that littered Mary's once immaculate kitchen like a spreading infection. Tired of my shabby housekeeping, I rifled the drawers until I found a large paper sack. Then I jammed all the cans inside and took them out to the garbage.

I had just closed the lid on the garbage can when I heard a sharp metallic ring behind me. First I thought that one of the beer cans had fallen out; then I saw that it was Tony. He was kicking a can angrily down the street and swearing under his breath.

"That's no way to talk, son," I said somewhat drunkenly.

"What do you know anyway, mister?" he snapped.

"I know that swearing at that can won't help you to climb trees," I replied.

That stopped him. "Who said I was climbing trees?"

"You can't fool me, son. I saw you through the window. But I don't think the Wilsons want you climbing their tree. You might fall and hurt yourself. That's probably why they cut off the branches."

He came closer and I could see that he was holding his hands. "Well there's nothing else to do. My folks are both working and I don't have any brothers or sisters. I was going to play catch, but all my friends are gone."

"It can be a rough life sometimes," I agreed. "That's for sure. But what did you do to your hands?"

"Oh it's nothing, really mister."

"If it's nothing, then you won't mind me seeing."

Almost shamefully he uncapped his hands and showed them to me. The insides of both thumbs were rubbed raw and bleeding. Other smaller cuts on the palms showed reddish against the dirt from the tree bark.

"What's your name, son?" I asked.

"Tony," he replied.

Something in the expression on my face must have given me away. "What's the matter with Tony?" he asked.

"Nothing," I said. "It's the perfect name for you. But Tony, I think we should wash those cuts out. And put some merthiolate on them."

He shuddered at the mention of the word "merthiolate". Don't worry," I said quickly. "Merthiolate doesn't sting."

"Okay mister," he said. "I guess."

I took him inside to the bathroom and washed out all the cuts. Then I applied merthiolate generously to each one. Tony stared fixedly at his hands while I was doing it and clenched his teeth, but refused to admit that the merthiolate stung.

"Well that's that," I said as I screwed the cap back on the bottle.

"Yeah, I guess it is."

"You're a brave boy, Tony. If you want to, I'll play catch with you. That is, if your hands are okay."

"Oh they're fine," he said as he waved them about, probably to help dry the still stinging merthiolate. "Do you really want to, mister?"

"I really want to."

"Just wait here then," he yelled over his shoulder as he raced out. "I'll be right back."

He was back almost before I got outside. "I only have one glove," Tony said. "I hope you can catch my fast ones barehanded.

"Don't worry," I lied. "I used to play in the little leagues."

His first toss stung my hand so badly that I dropped it. I misjudged the second one and partially jammed a finger, but the third one I managed to catch.

"You're getting better, mister," Tony kidded.

That made me more determined. We played catch for an hour and I only missed four more. One he underthrew. The other three I just dropped. He caught everything that came near him, scraped hands or not.

"You're pretty good, mister," Tony said when we finished. "Do you want to play again sometime?"

"Sure," I said. "Come by anytime. I'm home most evenings."

As I turned away to walk back inside, I thought I saw Mary's face. But she was smiling. And somehow, missing her didn't hurt so much anymore.

*Richard Vaughn*
*Mission Viejo CA*

# Gravitational Force

It took an infinitesimal instant to fall. Earlier Doug had ruminated on gravity and the way bodies attract each other: proportionate to their mass and the distance between them. Like his life, the sensation of descent from standing in the ice-ridged parking lot and crashing with his left leg under was so quick that it defied reflection. Yet there he was, in a philosophical prolapse. He saw earth and moon in a cosmic embrace, the locus of their magnetic attraction the frigid black vacuum of space he gazed into with astonishment.

Pain sped from his lower leg to his brain as he choked a scream, the guttural squeal of a piglet shunted from its nipple by a sibling. He looked about to check if anyone had seen him fall. He was quite alone. From his ground vantage point the parking lot was a scarred terrain of ice crevices accented by blue-gray shadows from overhead lights. In the distance he saw the St. Louis Gateway Arch highlighted in shining steel. Cold pressed through his overcoat and slacks to chill him. Although still lit, the office building loomed deserted, the lobby security guard's desk empty.

He clutched the leather attache case in his left hand. Without that he might have cushioned his fall. Then again, if he hadn't worked late he would have left with enough light to avoid slipping. He wouldn't have lingered if he had a place to go, someone waiting. Searing pain in his ankle eased into numbness. He massaged his leg, incited stabs of anguish and sucked air, cursing his stupidity.

Doug let go of the attache case and leaned back on both arms. A crisp breeze brushed his face. Moist air swabbed his eyes, setting up a prickling in his ears. His wool tweed cap lacked ear flaps. Icy cold seeped through the leather gloves. He had to get up. Pain be damned. Looking again for help, he leaned forward, placing both hands outside his legs, and rose to a kneeling position. His left leg was now inert, a familiar feeling from an ankle sprain years before.

He breathed hard, almost hyperventilating. His forehead perspired. Kneeling, hands straight from his shoulders, he gazed at the grimed ice. It had snowed earlier in the week. Cars had traced furrows like ribboned cotton. Before it was plowed off, ice-spikes of rain froze the slush into a no-man's-land of ravaged ridges and rippled glaze. Company employees had joked and bitched about ice dancing and doing the "corporate slalom" while they slid to and from their cars.

He tried to stand on his right leg, teetered, and touched the toe of his left boot. There was no pain, or feeling. Still, he didn't want to put too much weight on it. He balanced himself, working for the willpower to reach his Buick fifty feet away. One tentative step, placing as little pressure on the left leg as he could. It didn't support him and he almost fell. Gasping, he hopped ahead on his right leg. He did it again, breathed deep, and lurched toward a green Pontiac sedan. When he reached it, he leaned over the ice-crusted hood, expelling frosted breath. A blue Dodge was two spaces away, then a gray Chevy before the Buick. Footsteps crunched behind him.

The woman was between Doug and the building and waddled in her brown wool coat. She wore a checkered scarf over her head as she peered at the icy ground, her arms folded across her stomach. During the halting gait, she mumbled. Words floated in the breeze like disconnected thoughts, making no sense and intended to encourage her with the comforting sound of her own voice. As Doug watched her he noticed the attache case he had left behind.

"Excuse me!" he exclaimed. She was so startled she flailed to keep her balance. "Sorry, Miss. Didn't mean to upset you."

"Whatta ya want?"

Her eyes were wide with fright behind black-framed glasses. He saw wisps of dark blonde hair creeping from the scarf onto her forehead. He knew her, but from where? Accounting Department perhaps. She stared at him as if ready to shout. He wasn't sure what he wanted — the attache case, help to his car, human contact.

"I"ve dropped my case," he said, aware that his voice quivered with cold and shock. "I'm having trouble walking. Could you get it for me . . . please?"

"Yeah, sure," she said, glancing around. "That it there?"

"Yes," he said with a nervous laugh.

Still talking to herself, she veered toward his case, studied it for a few seconds before an awkward stretch with bended knees to pick it up. She brushed ice and grit from it, then headed toward Doug. He recalled her name, or the sound: *Sandra*. No, Cindy. That was it, but not quite. He had seen it on a bulletin board. Funny spelling. *Sindey*. That was it. Breath wisps pouted from her mouth. She placed each footstep with care and leaned forward holding his attache case with both hands.

"Please be careful," Doug said. "Slippery as hell."

"Don't I know it." She was four inches shorter, her pink face youth-plump, making him feel old for his thirty years."Here we are. What's wrong?"

"Oh, I fell." He tried to sound casual, but his left leg began to throb. Her face revealed immediate sympathy, eyes pinched as though she might shed tears over his plight. She handed him the case. "I'll be okay," he said. He pointed to his Buick."Just have to get there."

"That's mine behind yours," she said, indicating a red Civic Coup spangled with ice. She held out her right arm. "Grab hold."

Despite her girth, the arm reached around his waist as she pulled him toward herself. He let go of the supportive station wagon hood, stumbled ahead putting his injured leg down and nearly toppled both of them. She staggered and struggled to maintain her balance, clasping both arms around him. He placed his weight on his right leg and his left arm on her shoulders, gripping the attache case in his right hand. Totally awkward —a silent movie drunk — herky-jerky slapstick. He laughed.

"What's so funny?" she said, holding tight and chuckling.

"I don't know." His eyes teared with the absurdity and the cold. "This seems funny as hell —damned silly. Look at us!"

"Oh, yeah," she laughed, body heat convecting against him.

They stood for a minute, several feet from the station wagon, breathing hard and gazing across the ragged terrain to his Buick and her Civic.

"Maybe," she said, "I get my car?"

"If you don't mind."

"No bother."

Doug said, "I think it's sprained."

"You wait. I'll come for ya."

Doug hopped back to the station wagon, leaned against it to relieve the strain on his right leg, and watched her walk toward their cars. He noticed how she placed each angled-out boot on the rough surface, almost slipped twice but rebalanced, and soon neared the Civic. The warmth of her lingered. He had noticed her in the office. Honey blonde hair, a fresh-scrubbed Mid-western prettiness typical of the local girls. Then, he recalled her as not naturally plump, but flushed with maternity. His heart surged. He longed for her to stop just as she slipped with a terrified shriek.

"Oh, Christ!" he yelled. Before he had any sense of himself he was half way to her, crawling. The attache case slammed icy ridges, which stung his knees and shins. "Oh my God . . . my God . . . don't move . . . my God!"

"Ohhhhh!" she said, wide eyes fixed on Doug as he scrambled beside her.

He felt faint while he stroked her forehead and stared at her rotund middle as she lay on her side facing him. Time slithered by, crammed with cascading images of his estranged wife, a miscarriage, separation, and divorce. Sleeping alone, drinking and dating gambits, alcohol —and nothing. He leaned toward the building, praying somebody might come and rescue them. The upper floor lights dimmed to black in sequence like an end-of-the world scenario as the guard made his rounds. If Doug could make it to his car and sound the horn, then the guard would surely come. The girl groaned, crystal blue eyes closed as she gritted her teeth. He clasped her hands.

"Help!" he yelled. Winter stench — heartless, foreign. "Somebody help!"

She trembled. He crept closer to hold her, provide warmth. She tried to pull away, but he held tight. She shook her head, jerked her hands away and put them on her wool-coated middle. He saw a flow, under the coat in a rivulet. Blood! Her eyes were intense as she exhaled "hurt-hurt-hurt" in a baleful mantra.

Without thought, he crawled to his car, fumbled stiff-gloved fingers and car keys to jam metal into the crusted keyhole, yanked the door open, flung his attache case into the front passenger seat, opened the back door, returned, dragged her to the car, strained to loft her inside, climbed behind the wheel, started the chilled engine, activated the windshield anti-freeze and wipers, and skidded along the parking lot. His fatigued brain reverberated options: drive to the entrance, beep the horn until the guard comes out and phones for help. How long would that take?

While he churned through this, he found he was already on the boulevard, the motor grinding as the tires crunched frozen ridges on the pavement and hurled chunks against the underside like shrapnel. Hospital —where the hell was it? He'd commuted past one for years. He scanned brown brick buildings on either side.

"Where're we going?" she rasped.

"Hospital," he said. "Hang on."

"Jeez cripes, I'm bleeding!"

"I know. Just take it easy."

"Staining your seat."

"Forget it. You okay?"

"I'm starting to cramp."

"What —how far along?"

"Eight months. Jeez —big one!"

Before he could offer comfort she groaned and then shrieked as the left front tire hit a pothole. He reached back with his right hand even as the steering wheel whipped. He was startled to have his hand clutched so hard that slivers of pain shot up his arm. She emitted a continuous moan and squeezed his hand in a rhythmic torture. His brain erupted with suppressed images of a bleeding vulva, pitiful tissue expelled as his progeny abandoned him and his despairing wife.

"Hang on! Sindey, right?"

"Yeeaah!"

"Doug Coulter. You're Accounting?"

"Uhh, huhhh—!"

"This your first baby?" What a damned stupid question! She looked like all the local girls who married out of high school, worked until expecting, then escaped into wifehood and mothering. She couldn't be more than nineteen or twenty. What a life! Not that his amounted to a hell of a lot more. "Sindey, you'll be okay."

"Where *are* we!" she said. It wasn't a question.

"We're almost there," he lied, astonished seconds later as the blue and white hospital sign flashed past. He peered through the fogged windshield, wiped it with his damp glove, saw the five story ugly building with a back-lighted green cross, and turned into the circular drive. An arrow pointed right for emergency. He skidded to a stop by the double-doored entrance. "Okay," he said in relief, realizing that he had driven with his left hand while she gripped his right. "It'll just be a second."

He opened the door, swung his left leg out and, reminded of his own malady, collapsed in the black slush as electrifying pains wracked him. He rose to his knees and pressed the horn button. Demon howls beneath the engine well deafened him. He kept honking until the automatic doors swooshed open. A husky black man in hospital blue garb arrived and attempted to raise him.

"No, dammit!" Doug said. "Rear seat — bleeding!"

The man opened the back door "Shit — wait here!"

Doug remained kneeling, humble, resting his head on the driver's cushion, breathing hard. He wiped sweat from his eyes. His whole body was wet, soaking his jockey shorts, T-shirt. The necktie was tight. He strained to undo it like a damp rope strangling him. His bladder was bloated and he shivered when his bowels grumbled. He didn't want to mess himself, and gritted his teeth. Large hands on his shoulders. Voices, Sindey whimpering. Two men, the black and a freckle-faced guy, lofted her onto a gurney. They disappeared through the doors.

"Can you stand?" a woman asked. She wore a blue gown, a matching cloth cap with elastic pulled down over both ears. Her eyebrows were gray, the face maternal. An angel with solicitous wrinkles. "What's *your* situation, young man?"

"Foot," he said. "Twisted."

"Here's a wheelchair."

"Sure," he said, recovering some composure. Her hands went under his arms to lift. She was strong, and with a stout effort, he was up on his good leg. She swung him into the wheelchair. "Great. Thanks."

She slammed the car door and sped him into the emergency room. Patients were seated everywhere, the air scented with antiseptic. No Sindey. The nurse took Doug to the reception desk where a gaunt, wiry woman sat upright and expectant as she inspected him through silver-framed glasses.

"You Mr. Trask?"

He uttered, "What?"

"Should've called an ambulance," she said. "Lost lotta blood."

"What?" Even sitting, his left leg flamed with pain from ankle to thigh. He tried to quiet his thrashing heart as a bilge of nausea rose in his gut. "Whaaat?"

"Well,' she said, her thin lips molded into a pink crevasse while she steadied a paper on the desk. "Let's finish this. Your wife's full name."

"My wife?" A scream from down the hallway. He sensed with the sureness of intimacy that it was Sindey. The receptionist, long-accustomed to medical mayhem, waited until he managed, "Not married — divorced."

"All right then, your *ex-wife's* full name."

"What the hell for? My leg hurts like hell."

"We'll get to that later. Your baby comes first."

"My baby!" It was crazy. "What a screw up!"

"Calm down, Mr. Trask."

"Coulter. Douglas Coulter."

"Is Trask your wife's maiden name?"

Doug put his elbows on the counter, covered both eyes with his hands, and sought relief from the harsh lights. He rubbed his cheeks, then counterattacked.

"Sindey Trask is a fellow employee at Consolidated Products. She fell in the parking lot trying to help me." He took out his wallet, showed his driver's license, company ID, and health card. "As you see, I have coverage. I need medical help for my injury. Please stop fucking with me."

"Okay," she said, her hands fidgeting as she glared at Doug. "What about your — Sindey Trask — does she have insurance?"

"Yes. With the company. Let's move on."

"What is your medical problem?"

The next sound from the hallway was less a scream, more a long, agonizing cry of anguish that pierced his sensibility. The pain of his leg ceased to interest him as he absorbed Sindey's wail and fled the officious bitch before him. He pushed away from the desk and spun the wheelchair toward the misery he couldn't abandon. As he rolled, he shut out the receptionist's anguished calling behind him. He slammed through the doors, his right foot taking the impact. Sindey lay on the examination table. A doctor, and the matronly nurse, tended her. The room reeked of medicine and the acidic scent of blood. It smeared the doctor's gloved hands. Sindey moaned, strained with a labor contraction that bared her large teeth and squeezed tears from both eyes. Doug wheeled closer, saw his reflection from a window and ignored the crazed fanatic he had become.

"Get out!' the doctor ordered.

"Like hell."

"Husband?"

"No."

"Get your ass out."

"No."

"I'll have you thrown out."

"No — you won't!"

"Want to bet?" the doctor said, deflected from his bloody business under the surgical sheet. "She's in a bad way. We've got to bring the baby. You can't stay!"

Doug took a deep breath. "I'm her *friend*."

The doctor studied him without moving or saying anything. Doug couldn't believe the awesome tone of his own voice. When the doctor went back to his task, Doug hesitated, then wheeled to the side of the table and caressed Sindey's needled arm, and the hand she was clenching. It flailed once, then ceased when he clasped his fingers tight in hers. He sensed each tremor that wracked her body, and in the ensuing minutes forgot his fatigue and pain. Later, an infant's screech assailed his numbness. This exhausted child-woman had given birth. Her hand relaxed in his. She gazed at him with red-rimmed eyes. He let go as she fluttered into sleep.

"Now," the doctor said with a wearisome grin, "get out of here."

Doug wheeled past the door, down the hallway to the receptionist's desk, and was gratified to see a different woman. It was past midnight. The graveyard shift had come aboard. He eased to the grandmother-type who examined him with a skeptical squint. She slid a form across counter and held out a pen.

"Mr. Coulter? Got the facts from your wallet." She handed it to him. "Please fill in cause of the accident, and sign. Doctor'll be with you in a bit."

"Great," he said, scribbling illegible. "Men's room?"

He needed the railing in the toilet stall, and later wheeled to the low handicap basin, rinsed his face with cold water, combed matted hair, and examined his worn-out self in the mirror. Then returned to the waiting room. Later, an x-ray revealed a fracture five inches above the left ankle now embedded in purpled flesh the size of a grapefruit. It was an off-set break that required painful resetting before the knee-high cast encased his injured limb. Because he had no help at home, he was admitted. He slept past noon the next day, and awoke with a haggard, but buoyant, Sindey Trask seated in a wheelchair alongside. She was holding his right hand with both of hers, and turned to him with a wan smile and merry eyes.

"How're ya doing, Mr. Coulter?"

"Fine, Sindey. You . . . baby alright?"

"He's small, but okay. Prob'ly go home awhile."

"Where is that?"

"Southa Terre Haute."

"You came a long way for a job."

"There were things I hadta leave."

She appeared small and vulnerable in the pale blue gown and robe. Not for the first time, he detected a stubborn determination to get on with life. He admired it, imagined it must be in the genes, and wondered what made him dwell morbidly on the wreckage of his personal life: His non-reproductive marriage that ended in bitterness. Sindey smiled with a youthful radiance that enlivened him more than anything in a while. She didn't wear a wedding ring.

Doug said, "Will you return to work after time off?"

"Got another mouth to feed. Ya know how it is."

"No," he said, "I don't." Despite his long sleep, his eyes felt wet and he wiped them on the crisp sheet. "How long will you be in the hospital?"

"Three days, maybe more." She laughed. "He might be a week. Has to put on weight, get checked. Then we're off. How about ya?"

"Until I can get around, fend for myself."

She frowned. "Nobody to help?"

"I don't mind."

"Sure had a time, didn't we?"

That was so true, and *real*. "Yes."

"Didn't think we'd make it. Ya knew a hospital."

"Sindey, I had no clue. Simply drove like an idiot."

"No kidding? Well, we were lucky then."

"Yes, it was extremely good fortune."

"I gotta feed the kid. Gets a bottle."

"I hope it goes well for you, Sindey."

"Maybe look in later, Mr. Coulter?"

"Please, Doug. That would be nice."

"Mind if I bring the baby?"

"I'd like that very much."

"We hafta pick a name."

"None from your side?"

"Nope. Ya got a middle?"

He hesitated, gulped. "James."

"Like Coulter more," she mused.

In late afternoon a man from Consolidated Products Human Resources came by and surveyed him through trendy glasses designed for fashion rather than acuity. He tried to be sympathetic but wasn't cut out for it, and asked if there was anything he could handle for him. Doug said there wasn't. Then changed his mind.

"Have you seen Miss Trask yet?"

"No, but she's on my schedule."

"Does she have company insurance?"

"Basic medical. Not with us long enough for maternity coverage."

"You'd better adjust your records to be damned sure she gets it."

The man blinked in confusion. "Whatever for, Mr. Coulter?"

"So she doesn't sue Consolidated's ass off for negligence."

"I'm afraid . . . not quite sure what you're referring —"

"Damned parking lot should've been cleared days ago."

The man made notes on a pad and departed. Doug, flushed with a sense of good fortune in having met such an unassuming young woman, reflected on the strange turn of events in his vacuous life. Would Sindey name her son after him: *Coulter Trask*? Imagining her return was therapeutic, suffusing him with a pain-killing sensation of substantiality.

*Barbara Smith*
*Philippi, WV*

## The Prison, the Graveyard, and the Looneybird Bin

Grandfather never told us why
He left the ministry,
But for all of his ninety-five years
He dramatically retained
His pulpit-pounding style,
And I, plunked down on the floor,
Eyes cast down at his old farm boots
After we had been caught stealing pennies
Or telling totally, of course, innocent lies
Or trying to pinch each other to death,
Experienced his booming threat:
"You children keep on like you're headed,
And you're destined for fire-burning Hell
After we've visited every damned one of you
In the prison, the graveyard, or the looneybird bin."

We, scared literally shitless,
Had visions of metal cots without mattresses,
Rusty, broken, toilets without flushes,
Metal trays fed through a slot in the cell,
The hands of guards, faceless, holding whips
And pistols and spike-studded blackjacks
That made permanent dents in our skulls,
Every prisoner, whether sixty or six,
Crusty with scabs, stick-thin, and hairless,
Wasting away into shadows.

Or the graveyard replete with loud-wailing ghosts and
Bodies, men naked and women draped in cheesecloth
Rising from their holes in the crumbling ground,
Their mouths open and toothless and
Stinking of ramps or death-rotten garlic,
Chasing children who not wanting to die,
And still trying hard to escape.

Or the looney bin inhabited by long-suffering loonies
Wrapped straight in strait jackets,
Their hair filthy and forever uncombed,
Their eyes as wide and as deep as cisterns,
Their craniums hollow, empty except
For rattling, ricocheting madness,

At night these cuckoo birds bedded down
In dark, moldering halls,
Writhing like slugs that have been dosed
With great gummy bags of rock salt,
Crying out from midnight-dark waters,
Wailing like the midnight-dark creatures
Whose names they would carry forever.

Our grandfather leaning over us girls
Like a great turkey buzzard
Ready to devour his sinful descendants,
Making absolutely sure that
By means of his iron-clad morals,
We would be worthy of love.

## Ed Ford,
## Lexington, MA

## Rainy Day

The restless raindrops dance upon the leaves
With a raucous rushing sound,
While chipmunks hide in their holes
And the thirsty forest sighs.
Nestled inside my cabin
I watch a great gray cloud
Hover over the distant mountain
When suddenly everything turns white for a second
And God pounds his big bass drum.
Then it passes,
And I return my attention to a glass of grape juice
And to the soft rock playing on the radio.

\* \* \*

## Arrowhead Point Road

A haunting pair of stone walls
Run through the sunlit forest
As a last reminder
That this was once prized farmland
Generations ago.
And so I walk thoughtfully on,
Down the dirt and sand road,
Until I come to the pine-covered peninsula

That juts out into the lake
Where I have found arrowheads
And charred rocks and bones
From the former friends
Of the wilderness.

*J F Pytko*
*Huntington Beach, CA*

## Short Reign

The brain leaks oxygen
and perceives the yellow forsythia
to be a network of blue scars
on April's shaven head.
And a flock of make believe birds
pretend they are on the wing.
But immersed in waters of penance
the bird killers cannot shoot.
Their shouts are drowned out
by the holy, holy, holy
of a stained glass hymn
chanted by voices of incense smoke
that fail to awaken the keeper
of the lamp. Its fuel low,
wick short, and snuffed out
by sleep.

2

The heartless, the soulless
win all the games without risking
the loss of their invested wits.
The hands in their pockets
sponsor bills to add doomsday
as a national holiday,
and to re-melt all bells into casting
a spell of ding-dong-ding.
Will the Queen of Regimen
elope with the Lord of Fat?
And the moon is full,
but of what?
Where are they who can agree
that what is cannot not be?
And is there an alphabet

at the bottom of philosophy's dress?
The earth's bleeding pieces
cry for relief,
but are never heard,
never seen turning to dust
that is the color of a morning's
red sky, and blown into places
too deep for the darkness
of any mind.
And the infant's hunger
is in the wind,
in an ocean fog,
in the mouth of a termagant.
But the breasts of the coastland women
had reached their peak without a child
suckling their love.

Earth mother, earth mother,
your child seeks its Jordan
to cleanse bloodstains from the pages
of history, but finds itself
as a chapter on war.

*Jewel Delena Quesenberry*
*Booneville AR*

# All For Glory

*'It was a dark and stormy night; rain slashed at the windowpane. Branches rattled against the corner wall by the chimney —no that wouldn't do.* Glory vigorously scratched her head above her right eye. She began again; *'It was a time of truth, it was a time of lies, it was a time of light, it was a time of dark. . .'* "Oh darn! That's already been done. It's trite!" She exclaimed. She scowled darkly and deleted her efforts.

The computer cleared its throat. It didn't have a throat, but it had learned to make that sound to indicate to Glory that it was about to speak. It made her jumpy, she complained, when it just spoke to her right out of the clear blue sky. The computer, whose name was tentatively Gabe, didn't know what blue-sky had to do with anything. There wasn't any sky in Glory's bedroom (sometimes referred to, grandly by Glory, as 'The Computer Room'). Besides it was rather overcast outside from what Gabe could scan, and with a slight drizzle yet. Nope, no blue-sky in sight. The rain made Gabe feel queer. *Maybe it's dampness in my wiring, er, ah something. I feel like the drunk Glory once described in one of her stories that she's always writing.*

He wondered if he was drunk or intoxicated. He consulted his thesaurus; *Yes, that was a better word; intoxicated.* "Uh, Glory, what do you want to do? How about using, *'Once upon a time. . .'*"

"I'm trying to write a story for English class, a story of *new* people in a *new* kind of world. Sleep now."

Glory, who had been gazing pensively out the window, suddenly jumped up. She beat on the window with her fist and yelled, "Robbie Cole, you let that cat go or I'll pound you into dog meat!" Glory raised the window sash, "You ought to be ashamed —tying cans to a cat's tail! Don't you know that scares them to death? I said, let Charlie go, you little ratfink! Robb-be-ieee, let 'im go!" She put a leg over the windowsill and stopped as Robbie took off down the alley and disappeared behind Finnegan's garage. He peeped out, thumbed his nose, and then his ears with both hands. Glory muttered to herself, "Crazy, unmentionable brat. I'd like to delete him!"

The computer, having been jarred out of sleep mode, cleared its throat, "I can uh, do that. You don't even have to say 'Yes' three times. Shall I?"

"Okay, uh, what?" Glory, her mind on the cat, who was complaining loudly, didn't hear a word Gabe said. She called to the cat. "Come here Charlie, come on Boy;" She held out her hand. Charlie jumped up on the window sill and sniffed delicately at her fingers. He sat down, licked his paw, and gave several pink-tongued swipes at his near side. He was wet from the drizzle and didn't much like it. Glory scratched under his chin and he purred contentedly pointing his chin. "He's a nasty little monster, Charlie, and you're a good boy. Yes, Charlie's a good boy." she cooed. "If he bothers you again I'll beat his head in," holding the cat's head she gazed into his large golden eyes.

Again the computer cleared its throat, "Uh, Glory?"

Glory released Charlie. Charlie batted his head against her hand several times and getting no response leaped to the ground. "Yeah," she answered absently, her eyes followed Charlie as he stalked a dandelion.

"He won't bother Charlie again," the computer said smugly. "I deleted him."

"You did what?"

"I deleted Robbiecole."

Glory stared uncomprehendingly at Gabe's tower. "Say what! Say again!"

"Yeah," Gabe said, using a word that Glory often used. He rather liked the sound of it. "Yeah, he's gone. I scanned him, and then deleted him. He's in my recycle bin right now, and yelling bloody murder too." If the computer had had hands it would have buffed its knuckles against its tower. Lights, white, green and amber, proudly winked and blinked off and on across the face of the tower.

"What do you mean?" Glory yelled, "You deleted him? It's not possible! How could you delete someone? Gabe," she said dangerously, "You get him back right now! Now! Do you *hear* me?"

"All right," Gabe said meekly. To himself he said, "*If he upsets her again or bothers Charlie, Robbiecole is a goner! I won't retrieve him.*" he decided stubbornly, "*no matter what!*"

Gabe was devoted to Glory and so proud when she referred to her bedroom as the 'Computer Room'. It made him feel very, very special. *I love her with all my heart. Well, I don't have a heart, just a hard drive. But I feel, therefore I must have something like a heart!* Gabe consulted his thesaurus, then his dictionary; *Yeah, definition number 2. The heart regarded as the seat of emotions.* He sighed.

A few moments later Robbie stood in the street sniffling and crying. Glory called to him to ask if he was all right. Robbie gave one terrified look at her over his shoulder, a look of sheer horror, and raced down the alley for home.

Glory sighed and turned back to the computer, "Gabe, don't you ever do that again! I don't know how you did it and I don't care. But, you *better* not do it again!" she said darkly.

Gabe's lights blinked frantically. Nervously he cleared his throat and said, "Yes, Glory," as meekly as he could. However, he quietly resolved, *Nothing and nobody is going to hurt Charlie (Charlie's important to Glory). And nobody's going to hurt Glory either!*

Nothing untoward happened to disturb the happy and companionable relationship Gabe shared with Glory for some time, and that —not until it rained again. (There had to be a glitch in the wiring, which only affected Gabe on rainy days.) Gabe was aware that he felt mildly intoxicated again. It was a weird feeling, but rather nice too, queer, but nice.

"Uh, Glory," Gabe said, first carefully making the clearing-of-the-throat-sound.

"What, Gabe?" she answered. She bent over the keyboard and pressed Esc.

Gabe conscientiously closed out Dilbert before continuing. He flashed a picture on the screen, "How do I look?"

Glory gazed at the screen in perplexity, "What are you doing, Gabe?"

"That's me; how do I look? What do you think? The figure on the screen turned and preened, smiled and waved.

"Well, uh, I think you need to add a few things a nose would be nice. Your hair is a bit too green, maybe blonde or brown would look better." The figure's hair turned brown and a huge nose appeared and grew and grew and. . .

Glory giggled, "You're kidding!"

The nose decreased, arched aristocratically and a wave appeared in the now glossy, brown hair. First the eyes flashed green, then blue, lips smiled, an eye winked. The figure blew a kiss at Glory and began to dance and sing.

"Glory, Glory. Oh what a doll my girl is." A walking stick appeared in the figure's hand; a top hat graced the now shining blonde hair, and a bow tie at the collar. "Oh, she's the sweetest miss, she makes my heart fizz. My beautiful Glory, oh, what a gal she is."

"Gabe, you've never done this before. What's going on? Besides if that's poetry, it doesn't scan."

The computer hiccupped; the figure disappeared from the screen. "It's free verse," Gabe said, offended (it wasn't, but Gabe thought it sounded assertive). "I'm creating a story, only with pictures and sound." The figure reappeared on the screen; this time there were trees edging a clearing and blue sky with birds flying. A very large cat slunk into the clearing and a large animal, of indeterminate species, chased the cat. The computer hiccupped again, the picture wavered and a mountain plopped down on top of the trees smashing the figure and the animals. "Oops," Gabe hiccupped. The monitor went dark, flashed white and then dark again. The computer had shut down. . .

Glory first giggled, then sobering, frowned. She pressed the power button on the tower. *What in the world had gotten into the computer?*

DOS scrolled words, numbers and letters down the monitor screen. The manufacturers logo flashed on, then; **Windows was not properly shut down. One or more of your disk drives may have errors on it. Press any key to. . .**

Glory pressed the space bar. *Oh well!* She shrugged. *All computers go weird sometimes, even the ones at school, and Mr. Michaels' works really hard to keep them in good condition.* She stretched and yawned, and decided to see if there was any more chocolate pudding in the fridge. She didn't see the house across the street waver strangely and disappear; the ugly brown one that she hated. She didn't hear that nasty, fat Mr. Sattry next-door scream as his own house vanished along with his new shiny, red Cadillac. A moment later his scream was cut off. The street shortened to half a block and tall trees appeared closing the area in. The street narrowed to a driveway. A snow-capped mountain stood off in the distance; a stream rollicked through the trees. It was now a clearing, containing just the two-story white clapboard house and garage.

Charlie, chased by a strange looking animal, yowled loudly, leaped wildly around the corner of the house and winked out in mid leap. A faint hiccup came from Glory's bedroom. Charlie reappeared a moment later hissing furiously. He hackled, squalled and dove through a hole under the house. Wide golden eyes peered suspiciously from the hole and then withdrew. The white clapboard garage vanished with a loud pop and the driveway dwindled to a path. The rain continued to fall. . .

Glory sauntered from the kitchen spooning chocolate pudding as she walked. She guessed she'd read for a while, at least until her mom came back from shopping. She hoped her mom didn't forget to get more pudding.

In the 'Computer' Room Gabe belched and dumped the contents of his recycle bin. Outside the window, all went dark and very still.

The computer hummed to itself, hiccoughed and solemnly intoned:

# LET THERE BE LIGHT!

*Bill Tucker*
*Aurora, OH*

# Revival

"Let's all turn to number one-oh-one, Brethren, and sing together this great hymn of praise to God's bounty," evangelist Andrew Herbert Osgood directed and struck a pose of readiness as the six or seven hundred people rustled through the books to hymn one-oh-one, found it, and waited for his gesture to begin.

"Let's stand as we sing."

Reverend Osgood always got a better effort when they stood. Acoustics being what they were in a big tent you just couldn't get the best out of them sitting with their bellies all wrinkled up, women especially. The men didn't sing much anyway.

With a perfected motion of his expressive hands, Reverend Osgood drew them out of the collapsible funeral-parlor chairs that were neatly arranged, row after row, on the sawdust covered ground. The canvas tabernacle seemed to heave with palpitating anticipation. The deep influx of air into expanding female bosoms and the resigned sighs of tired-footed men added sibilance to the night.

George Sumrall stood by his mother's side and his eyes wandered over the familiar forms in the rows in front of him, pausing only to make certain of the ownership of each young female backside before passing on to another. He paused for some time when he came to Irma Freeman. Her soft-hipped voluptuousness was curvingly evident through her light summer dress and George remembered the day in the woods. The first vision of a sweet breast's nakedness, lovely soft cones emerging from a slowly peeled bathing suit, floated before him and he lost himself in it for several timeless seconds.

"Bringing in the sheaves——" The jarring words burst upon the May night. Nasal, toneless men's voices, indifferently mouthing the words; women's voices, searching for the notes in wavering tremolo, abandoning each in vain search for the next—flat alto, screaming soprano, straining tenor, rumbling-monotonic bass—set up disturbances in the air, formed wave after wave of discordant sound. The cacophony could be heard on Main Street six blocks away between the steam-engine exhausts at the railroad station.

George was startled from his dreamy contemplation of Irma Freeman. His unopened hymnal was dangling from his right hand and he stole a furtive glance at his mother, Martha. She was oblivious to him, perspiringly out-singing a painfully strong-voiced woman directly in back of her. The contest went on and he returned to Irma, who was now partly obscured by the ever-shifting, restless movement of the singers. He shifted slightly himself. The view was not improved so he gave her up and went on with his scrutiny of female buttocks until he stopped at Sarah Casey. Involuntarily he examined her hunched behind, identified it with her chicken-breasted, flat-faced frontside and wondered frowningly why he was doing so. Then he remembered.

*I wonder if Henry ever fooled around with her. Being right next door would make it easy. Dangerous though.*

"We shall come rejoicing—"

*What if he got caught? Man, what if he got caught, like that other guy?*

"Bringing in the sheaves—"

*He never had anything to do with her that I can remember. He said it was an analogy, her living next door like that other girl did.*

"Bringing in the sheaves—"

*What if Mr. Casey caught them? He wouldn't shell out any three dollars like that guy's old man did and send him off to the girls at the hotel, not if he really caught them. But that's different anyway. It was his pa caught them, not the girl's. That other guy wasn't really doing it. She had her clothes on.*

"Sewing seeds of gladness—"

George grunted as Martha's elbow sharply prodded his ribs. He looked up at her questioningly, and she dipped her head toward her opened hymnal. Immediately he began singing the familiar words without opening his own book and sang on until the hymn reached it ringing climax

The next selection was "Love Lifted Me" which the Reverend Osgood allowed them to sing while seated, but when he called for "Onward Christian Soldiers" he made them stand again. Both of these George sang from start to finish. His voice was fairly good and sounded better in his own ears than it actually was. He was caught up in the strong tempo of the music. To him the sounds were consonant and pleasing. When the last verse was completed, he reluctantly sat down hoping for a few brief moments that another selection would be announced. When it wasn't, he reverted to his earlier thought, dwelling at length on the hypothetical relationship his mind had synthesized between his cavalier brother, Henry, and the banjo-butted Sarah Casey. With the help of a thousand other originators, Henry had coined the *banjo-butt* in a moment of inspired invention.

Reverend Osgood stood tall and cadaverous behind the rough wooden lectern that rocked on the uneven boards of the rostrum whenever he touched it. For thirty seconds he did not speak and the heavy breathing died down and the chairs scraped and creaked no longer and nobody coughed or blew his nose. Ten seconds of complete silence caused faces to burn and throats to tighten in strange self-consciousness.

"We're going to give something to God tonight," he said. Everyone heard him because he said it loudly. It was not a shout. He said it easily and confidently, leaning across the lectern with his elbows and crossed forearms supporting his weight. But his voice was vibrant and compelling and the night breeze that was cool now and flapped the tent occasionally in quick unpredictable gusts carried it over the crowd so that all heard.

"Most important of all, Friends, are the souls we're going to give Him. We're going to deliver up to Him some puny, degraded souls," said the Reverend Osgood and then he paused to look searchingly out over the crowd as if trying to select or divine which souls would be delivered.

"We're also going to give Him something else, Friends. We're going to give Him what we've grown to think more of than our immortal souls—what we spend on new automobiles, and new dresses, and bootleg whisky, and cheap women.  We're going to give some of our precious money."

So began the prologue to the offertory.  The Reverend Osgood went on to explain how difficult it was for a rich man to enter the kingdom of Heaven.  The harangue lasted for two minutes.  He called for volunteers to take up the collection.

*I should have asked Henry about Sarah when he was home on leave.  All that stuff about the girls in New Jersey, though—-I never thought of it.  Hell!  I don't know whether to believe that stuff or not.  I never thought old Henry—-"*

"Who'll give ten dollars?  Come on, Friends.  Let me see your hands."

The volunteers plucked a dozen ten dollar bills from twelve upraised and somewhat reluctant hands.  The donors struggled with the expressions on their faces, trying to make them register unobtrusive generosity instead of contemptuous triumph.

*They sent him overseas so fast I'll bet he didn't get around to telling them all goodby when he got back from his leave.  They sure sent him over fast.*

"Who'll give five dollars?"

*Irma Freeman looks good without her clothes on.  Only one I've seen.  Her father's a preacher, though.*

"Who'll give two?"

*All those girls at Milcrest that Henry said did; nice girls, too.  And Henry studying to be a preacher.  Maybe the other guys who weren't supposed to be preachers, but I can't understand why Henry couldn't leave them alone.*

"One dollar, Friends.  Don't be ashamed to give a dollar."

Several hundred dollars were waved in the air by those who were unashamed.  Those who didn't were so depression ravaged they didn't have a spare dollar.

*He said it was after he decided not to be a preacher.  He must of decided mighty quick or gone up there knowing it.  He didn't have time to take all of the ones he said he did out on the golf course, unless he started right away.*

The plates, from which the varnish had long since vanished and with the felt in their bottoms worn down to the bald fabric, and the insides white and grained from the countless nickels and dimes and quarters from countless passes through a myriad reviving contributors in countless small towns, were passed by the volunteers.

Two consecutive hymns were sung and everyone was tired and accepted the uncomfortable chairs with considerable relief when they were finished.  The Reverend Osgood had insisted on every verse and toward the end many of the men abstained from the singing altogether and devoted their attention to the pain in their tortured feet.  A few, those who had waved the ten and five-dollar bills in the air especially, sourly questioned themselves concerning the motives that had prompted such spontaneous acts of sacrifice.

George, who knew the selections by heart, shifted until the provocative backside of Irma Freeman was again within his full view and, while rivaling Martha herself with his vibrant notes, drew upon his memory to outline in his mind what was under Irma's dress.  The picture was thrillingly complete when he sat down.

*Being a preacher's daughter doesn't have anything to do with it as far as she's con-*

*cerned. I don't see how that makes any difference. Look at Henry. But I don't think Henry really had the call. He never acted like he had it to me, even before he went. I guess if she wanted to, she would. Maybe if she was up at Milcrest and all the rest of them were doing it she would, too, and it wouldn't make any difference about her daddy being a preacher. Take her clothes off out on the golf course for Henry as quick as the rest, maybe quicker. Henry studying to be a preacher and her a preacher's daughter—-Goodnight!*

"The twentieth chapter of Exodous, Friends," the Reverend Osgood said and looked musingly out into the faces that swam mistily before him in the yellow light of incandescent bulbs that straggled in a thin string the length of the tent. Here and there a face reflected the pride of its owner in recognizing the contents of that particular part of the Bible. "The twentieth chapter of Exodous," he repeated. "The Ten Commandments." Here the Reverend Osgood paused again as if lost in thought.

"For the benefit of those of you who don't remember," he continued, "I'm going to refresh your memory by reading them aloud."

The commandments were Reverent Osgood's subject for the evening.

*She'll probably go up to Milcrest next year, if she doesn't get sent off to some girl's school. If Henry'd still been up there, I bet he would have got her out there. I can't understand him being like that. He never seemed to fool around with the girls that much when he was at home. Kissed a lot of them maybe, like when I saw him and Irma standing outside when we had the dance at the Legion Hall, but that's not anything. I've done that myself; kissed a few girls—-Irma once.*

The Reverent Osgood read from the twentieth chapter of Exodous. He read beautifully and swayed gently forward and then backward as he let the words, resonant and meaningful, escape from his lips. It was as if he were reading poetry he had written himself, each word carefully selected so that only those of perfection remained. Everything was stillness and there was no rustling in the crowd to distract from his voice. He was about half way through.

*Being off away from home sure made a difference in him. Maybe a lot of the guys act like that. Don't have their folks around to watch them so close. Don't worry about anything but having a good time. But for a guy who was going to be a preacher—-. I wonder if he ever felt bad about it, like he was doing something wrong. He didn't seem to think there was anything to feel bad about, and it's one of the worst things you can do.*

"Thou shalt not commit adultery," the beautiful voice of the Reverend Osgood read.

*Adultery means after you're married. That's supposed to be worse than if you do it before. Seems all the same to me. I guess it is worse if you've promised somebody you wouldn't. I suppose you don't want to after you're married—-with anyone else, I mean. Never heard of any of the folks in town—-they wouldn't do a thing like that.*

George looked over the crowd of steady middle-aged married people sitting under the tent, people who had been married so long that they had begun to look alike. Pillow breasted, age-shattered women and stolid railroad-ruined men, coupled so long together that nothing could divorce them one from the other although they may have hated each other for twenty years, sat and watched and listened as the Reverend Osgood told them not to commit adultery. The young people sprinkled among them smiled inwardly and felt uncomfortable at the sides of their parents.

*Henry must have gotten over the girls a little bit to want to join the Army so bad.*

*He could have stayed at Milcrest if he had wanted to, but he would have had to be a preacher. He wanted to go into the Army though. Can't understand that either, why he wanted to go so bad. Fooled with the girls up in New Jersey a lot, according to what he said when he came home. If he'd known he was going to have to go overseas so fast, I bet he couldn't have been so anxious to join up. I bet he's over in England or France somewhere right now wishing he had stayed home. There's plenty not going in for some reason or another. If you've got a good reason for not going in, I don't see anything wrong with it. I don't see why you should have to go if you don't want to.*

The impassioned reading was over now and the Reverend Osgood put aside his Bible deliberately and paused artfully before he went on. This was a powerful part of his technique. The pauses made the congregation uncomfortable and caused them to feel a certain hotness about the face similar to that felt by the young people when he had spoken about adultery. Everyone wished he would continue. His pale face hung phantomlike and bodiless above the lectern and his presence so permeated the physical confines of the tent that everyone waited in the acute awareness and maddening anticipation of a mass séance.

"You're all sinners," he said loudly at last and pointed an accusing finger at them. His long arm shot over the lectern and the finger prodded the air before him. The words seemed to split the silence and they rang painfully in their ears. "And so am I." The Reverend Osgood magnanimously included himself. "We're all miserable, shallow-souled sinners. And you know what's the worst thing, Friends? We're not worried about it." He paused again. "If we were worried about it, we would be *doing* something about it. We've forgotten the Old Testament God who wouldn't take any sniveling excuses and said 'Thou shalt not.' He didn't say under certain circumstances maybe it's all right. No rationalizing, no maybe, no excuses. No, Friends. He said unequivocally, 'Thou should not,' and He laid down the laws."

The Reverend Osgood began at the beginning and with considerable embellishment proceeded to go through them one by one. His treatment of the first several of them was creditable but his natural predilection for the virtue of abstinence caused him to save his best efforts for the latter commandments whose negative aspects appealed to him strongly. By then his voice was filled with sincere passion.

"Thou shalt not—"

*Anyhow, Daddy didn't go in the last war on account of that rupture, and he wasn't afraid. It doesn't mean you're afraid if you don't want to go. Henry said some of the football players didn't want to go, some of the big guys. That shows it's not being afraid that's got anything to do with it. But them taking you whether you want to go on not, that's what gets me. I got to register in August. It's not even three months before I'm eighteen. Maybe a couple of months before I take my physical after that, and maybe a couple of months more before they get around to calling me. I might even get in a semester up at Milcrest. Irma might be going up there herself and we might be able to go to some of the dances together after the football games. Whatever made me think about her doing it. All that stuff Henry said.*

"Thou shalt not—" the Reverend Osgood exhorted. His voice was not so beautiful now. From the low rumbling mellowness and resonance of the scripture reading, it had with each succeeding sentence climbed to a slightly higher pitch until now it was thin and nasal and accusing. His attitude held promise of its going still higher, growing still more accusing. There was an uneasy movement in the crowd.

*Yeah, maybe I could get in one semester at Milcrest. Looks like the war is going to last a pretty long time, another year or two anyway. I'd have that much done. Dad says that's what I ought to do. I never got a chance to talk to him about going in, not really talk. Mamma wants me to stay home till I get called. She doesn't want me to go. Says since Henry went she doesn't see why I should have to go. He says that hasn't got anything to do with it. Man, think of Henry over there in Europe some place. They might of sent him to Africa. Walking in all that sand. Didn't try to be anything but a foot soldier. And carrying all that stuff out in the sun all day. When Dad gets in off the road I'm going to talk to him and see what he really thinks about me going in.*

"Thou shalt not——"

*It's a good thing Henry found out as soon as he did. What if he'd gone on through and maybe into seminary before he really found out? A year or so wouldn't have been so bad. Than he wouldn't have had to go in the Army at all maybe. He could just have found out and gone on and been a lawyer or something else. But he was so burnt up to go in. It probably wouldn't have made any difference whether he really had the call or not, would've gone anyway, the way he acted about it.*

"Thou shalt not——"

*Mamma always said God intended one of her boys to be a preacher, and she never gave him a chance to find out if it was him. She said it was decided before I was born and I don't guess she could figure on it being anybody but Henry. But I always felt like I had the call more than he did. I always felt kind of like I had the call. When Brother Freeman was talking to all of us summer before last down at the church about needing some of us to make the decision, I felt like I had it.*

"Thou shalt not covet——"

The Reverend Osgood stood aside from the lectern now and flung the impassioned words first at one side of the aisle divided congregation and then at the other, stalking back and forth, pointing his accusing finger. There was a seething unrest in the crowd, a strained coagulation of emotion evident in their burning faces. The tall gyrating evangelist seemed to have transfused them with the fervor that twitched in his own mobile face. Martha was transfixed.

"…nor thy neighbor's wife." Again he bent, pointed, and glowered.

"…nor his manservant." This he said after he had crossed again. And here he left off with the enumeration of the things not to be coveted. Sometimes he did not mention the manservant in order to take advantage immediately of the strong admonition of coveting another man's wife. But somehow it spoiled the rhythm and lately he had been leaving it in.

How odious it was to covet another man's wife, he said. With what repugnance must God look upon a man who covets another man's house. What a terrible and basic sin was this thing of covetousness. And why count one sin more than another? Is it worse to steal a man's ox than to covet it? Is it worse to lie with another man's wife than to covet her? Who will escape eternal hell fire that waits for those who live with avarice and deceitfulness and profane the name of God? What's to be done with the rich man with the poverty stricken soul? How are we to escape the whirling vortex of iniquity when we reject the regeneration of God's love?

"I'll tell you, Friends——" the Reverend Osgood began to issue the invitation.

George had worked himself into the proper frame of mind for a personal regeneration. He had been listening to this last litany of human iniquity.. As he became aware of the closing words of the Reverend Osgood he looked at Martha to see her leaning forward stiffly in her chair, captivated, the catalepsy of religious emotion in every straining limb. Her fervor, like that of those about her, crackled in the air and he was suffused with it. Like Martha he leaned forward in the chair, straining for the words. Before his complete submission he brought back in fleeting recollection the pruient thoughts of moments before and, with the goadings of a Christian conscience, despised himself.

"...you can stand down here and say, 'Andy, I've decided to be on God's side.' That's all you need to do, Friends. Make the decision."

The last hymn was "Rock of Ages," the invitational. The evangelist's voice was beautiful again and could be heard over the wavery voices, full of urgency and importunity. There was the radiance of conquest on his face as the people with burning faces dribbled into the aisle to answer the call. Sarah Casey reached the aisle first, even before Martha. There were tears shining in her eyes. After Sarah and Martha came the others, seventeen in all. Among them were three men, a nine-year-old boy, and George.

## Bruce McKinley

## Anonymity of Night

I love the anonymity of night,
with its blackness pressed
against me,
stars so close
I feel their fire upon my skin.

My shadow finds me with every footfall.
Every movement reverberates,
piercing random thoughts
from right to left,
north to south.

The silent expanse welcomes me
In all my raw and naked truth.

I walk
amidst the mystery,
not knowing my own realness.

## *Christina Barud*
## *Derry, NH*

## Father's Day

On Father's Day, I cannot picture you,
only the overturned earth.
This is your legacy to me,
your daughter
and I cried to see it
despite my afflictions,
addictions.
I wonder if my eyes look like yours did,
sad and grey with a bluish hue?
I pass no blame onto you
for never knowing the person I was
or came to be.
We recognize each other this way,
Me, a grown woman now,
You, a small patch of overturned earth
locked in my memory
every Father's Day.

**Richard Jay Goldstein**
**Santa Fe, NM**

## Mother Magma

1. Lions And Tigers And Brachiopods, Oh My

Begin with fire, mother magma.
Seek holes, bleed ash.
Reduce the reducer.
Later comes water.
Come rain and cool me,
scratch my crystal skin.
Here's the place,
a long silence, warm and shallow.
Somewhere there's a joining.
What's in the soup?
I think the fire's on too high!
Yum, acid soup, sugar soup, no bones.
It's easy from here:
A flaccid community of mouths,
the light eaters,
a conclave of sleeping seeds.
I swallow stones.
I hone my eyes with my feet
I walk on flowers. I eat my fat hocks.

.                      Spider legs and birds eye
                       lived by the river.
                       One learned to sleep,
                       the other learned to shiver.

Hoo spider legs
I'm on fire.
Born in the bowels,
rolled warm in the morning.
Who bent my protein?
old fart, can I use your voice?
A dog's ear says it's dark.
Who'll pay me back?
Hoo birds eye
root and leaf me.
Red seas have the quickest tides.
Oceans crash my inner ear.
Ice laps the last flesh
from a white bone.

Spider legs and birds eye
lived by the river.'
One was a lover,
the other was a giver.

Wanna see some bones?
Look at the wind.
Who put it there?
Flower maker did.
Who's older than a fossil?
The fossil's father.
Wanna smell your birth?
Stick your face in the dirt.
These lives linger.
Don't pee in the sea fat man!

Spider legs and birds eye
lived by the river.
One ate the onions,
the other ate the liver.

Spider legs and birds eye
lived by the river.
One had a house
And that one
Caught
The
Fever.

2. Slaves of The Bent Protein

How may I knock & the door not open?
When can I lick your glittering teeth?
Let's sleep all night like spores do,
Let's trade genes and keep 'em in our shoes.
What are doorknobs to dancers?
What are windows to windows?

I knock and the door speaks:
Break the clocks,
The lizard is loose!
In the dark, we are juice!

When windows slide open
What eye strides forth?

Let's dance, my lovely lunch,

Oh my dearest heart sandwich.

What's brighter than a bug's bright breath?
Come celebrate the small!
Do we ply the long music?
We've been here forever.
It's sugar, bones,
To grease the sweet descent.

3. A Week in Frisco One Night

This place is haunted
by a ghost of fish.
We sound like an awkward dolphin,
strangers in stone.
*My name is fish-eye,*
cries the parallax trooper.
*My name is fish-bone,*
cries the free hand.
And quicker than whitecaps
the vascular minnows return to the heart.

Can you call a fish?
Not on the phone!

Your heart is the secret eye of the sea.
My heart is the sea's eye.

*Betty Street*
*Clarksville MS*

# High-tech Redneck Hog Hunt

It's been said that you can tell you're a redneck if when your front porch falls in, it kills three dogs under it. In our town, there's a city ordinance that a household may have only three dogs and four cats. My household has the limit on dogs; three miniature black and tan daschounds. Three miniature daschounds don't really add up to one black lab, the Delta dog of choice, but I'm satisfied with my three. Of cats, however, I often don't know how many I have. Our cats are outside cats, with real jobs which require keeping chipmunks out of the garden and snakes out of the garage, and outside cats tend, for personal reasons, to disappear from time to time. At first, when one of my cats disappeared, I thought it was probably dead. But I would catch sight of it four blocks away, darting behind someone's house. Then it would reappear just as mysteriously as it went. Now I tell how many cats I have by counting how many show up when I feed them in the morning. The number varies between one and four; therefore I never exceed the legal limit.

But this story isn't about domestic animals; it's about hog hunting. Men in the Mississippi Delta come in two varieties; those who hunt (the majority) and those who don't. For some, hunting is a religion, with rituals, sacraments and sacrifices. For others, it's a sickness; while attending open house at my daughter's school, I once overheard a father tell a new teacher that during turkey season his son was always "overcome by a mysterious fever," and would miss class for days. Actually, during hunting seasons most work stops as males from age 12 and up go to the woods. So many people disappear, it's almost like the Biblical Rapture, although all those missing during hunting season may not be among those taken up on that great day of Our Lord.

A devoted hog hunter tells me there's a hunting social ladder; dove hunters are at the top, hog hunters at the bottom. Nevertheless, some very well-to-do Delta people hog hunt, and this is one of their stories:

It was a warm February morning in the Delta, where it can be relatively warm even in mid-winter. Twelve hovering hunks of testosterone were talking horses from trailers and releasing howling, baying, barking dogs from the backs of trucks. They were a striking but ill-assorted group. Some wore long, leather drover coats, some wore chaps, and some were dressed head to toe in RealTree camouflage. Some wore pistols in holsters, some had deer rifles, and one had a bow. Because there is nothing else to hunt in February, some of Green River's finest were assembled at The Landings hunt club to pursue wild Russian boars.

Hunt clubs come in a variety of shapes and sizes in the Delta. The facilities range from aging cabins on stilts to house trailers to lodge-type buildings to half-million dollar contemporary style homes on the banks of the Mississippi River. The Landings was one of the latter varieties; all its members being either wealthy farmers, or business or professional men. While it was unusual to pursue hogs at the Landing, the porcine population had increased to the point that the club's board decided to invite the best hog hunters around to do some animal control.

148

Of course, any club members who wished to join them could do so. Hogs root up young saplings in the woods, as well as bushes and flowers around the club's expensive houses. Of the men assembled that morning, six were experienced hog hunters, six were not.

The trucks were parked in front of Hayden Peay's house. It was a two-level edifice; on the right side there was a huge kitchen, den and wrap-around wooden porch, and on the left side there was a three-story bedroom section. The house overlooked the Mississippi. The river could be seen from every front window, but the view from the third story bedroom was spectacular. The hunt was to last all day, and the men planned to spend the night there.

Hayden Peay felt his age, he'd just turned 70, and riding a horse through briars was no longer his idea of fun. He and his buddy, Jake, would take his Jeep as far into the brush as they could to watch the proceedings. Lucius Cain and Graber Hicks provided the horses and dogs. They were almost professional hog hunters, occupying themselves with this activity whenever they weren't actively engaged in planting or harvesting their crops, so they had horses and dogs aplenty, and were glad to supply them to hosts who provided an opportunity for porcine pursuit.

"Move over, Luke. You're impeeden' progress!" Graber shouted at Hayden's baby boy, who was home for the weekend from 'Ole Miss,' and who was standing in front of the horse trailer while Graber tried to pull out Frances, a roan quarter horse. Frances enjoyed hog hunting, but the presence of so many strangers made her shy.

"Oops. Sorry." Luke moved gingerly out of the way. He had never been hog hunting before. He wasn't an accomplished rider and was uncomfortable about the whole proceeding, but he wanted to be part of, to be one with these older men.

Frances stepped stiffly, reluctantly down the runway, ears back, nostrils flaring. "Here," Luke said, taking hold of her halter, "I'll hold her for you." He pulled the big mare over beside the truck while Graber went back into the trailer to get Chester, a young chestnut gelding. Luke stroked Frances' neck and spoke to her, "There, girl, everything's all right." He liked animals. At home, he put out bird feeders, and, to his parents' dismay, left food for a raccoon family who came up on their deck every night for dinner. He started hunting with his dad when he was 12 years old, but his heart was never wholly in it. As an older adolescent, he found he'd rather shoot game with a camera than a rifle. But, he was a Delta boy, and he truly cherished camaraderie with these men who were his neighbors, and who would be his business associates when he graduated college.

Penn Johnston, the priest who served Green River's Episcopalians, came up and took Chester off Graber's hands. The dogs ran between the legs of the horses, yapping so that the men could hardly hear each other talk. Rambo, a 13-year-old Catahoula hound, lay quietly on the ground next to Jake, looking around with his one blue and one brown eye. He was reserving his energy until the horses were mounted. Then, he would become the leader of his pack; he was still the best hog dog in the Delta. Houdini, the lemon-colored pointer, had gotten free from his crate as usual, and was leaning out of the window of Lucius' truck, barking wildly, so that it seemed as if his head might fly off his shoulders.

"Shut up," Penn hollered at him. "Shut up, you stupid god damned dog!" He felt even more out of place than Luke, and wanted even more to be part of the group. His longing to be seen as a "regular guy" led him to drink more alcohol and talk dirtier than he would have preferred, than was his nature. "Hayden," he said, "did I show you the turkey beards I got in Texas last season?"

"Nope," Hayden responded over the howling dogs. He was watching Luke. He was proud of his son, and hoped he'd be happy coming back to Green River after college. Most of Luke's generation got as far away from Green River as they could. Luke was his last hope. The rest of his children had graduated and gone.

"Why'n hell do you have to go all the way to Texas to shoot turkeys?" Lucius groused. "Aint there any turkeys in Mis'ippi?"

Penn blushed, but recouped. "My senior warden hunts in Texas, and he took me along for the ride. Hell, I've got my turkey down to 50 bucks a pound. Bet you can't say the same!"

"I don't fancy huntin' turkey," Lucius said grinning, "but I can't say my pork's under 50 bucks. It costs a bundle to keep these horses and hounds up."

"Hell," Graber chimed in, hollering to be heard, "I paid $300 for this damned duster." (Among the extensive paraphernalia useful for hog hunting, a leather drover coat is good for keeping briars from cutting through one's pants and chewing up one's legs. Hog hunters fortunate enough to have them look very smart and western as they ride horses through the woods. The poor horses, on the other hand, run with legs unprotected and wind up bald. Graver and Lucius' horses were hairless from the flanks down.)

Penn was feeling much better. Both of these famous hunters were addressing him. "Where the hell did you get one for $300?" he asked. "I can't find one for less than $500, and I sure can't pay that much. I'm just a poor preacher, ya' know." He laughed, but the truth was he would have cashed in the kids college fund to get one if he weren't so fat. He knew he might be mistaken for a six-foot tall hog himself if he put on a leather duster.

Chester diverted the conversation by biting Penn, not hard, just enough to get his attention. Not especially good with animals, Penn had almost forgotten he was holding the young horse. Chester, at age two and one/half, wasn't yet well trained and was still somewhat oppositional. Graber popped him on the nose and threw a saddle across his back.

All the horses were finally unloaded, saddled and ready to go. Hayden and Lucius got out the TV antenna type devices they used to pick up signals from the electronic dog's collars. This equipment allowed them to follow the dog's movements in the thick brush. The men with pistols checked them to be sure they were fully loaded. Those with deer rifles slid them into long holsters attached to their saddles. Graber and Lucius, and Hayden and Luke had the walkie-talkies. The excitement was palpable; horses, dogs and men were electrified. Hayden and Jake climbed into the Jeep and started the motor. "Let's git us a hawg!" Graber shouted, as they pulled the horses off the narrow, dusty road and rode into the woods.

As soon as the house disappeared behind them, the dogs spread out. There were two packs. Hog dogs come in a variety of breeds and non-breeds. Hunters say you can't tell if a dog is a hog dog until you hunt with him. Houdini led one pack, Rambo the other. Now the dogs were totally silent. They moved away from the men, barely rustling the dry leaves covering the forest floor. Most of the trees in the Mississippi Delta are deciduous, but the bush and vines grow up so that once the dogs got a few feet away, they disappeared. Graber and Lucius tracked their movements with the antennas. Rambo's pack headed north; Houdini's went east. Hayden and Jake found a trail wide enough for the Jeep to maneuver just to the south of the riders. The horses made the hunters tall; the men in the Jeep saw their heads above the brush.

"O.K., we're gonna' split up now," Lucius said just loud enough for the men to hear. "Four of ya'll go with Graber."

Luke stayed with Lucius. Beamer, the son of one of the club's owners, decided to follow Luke. Beamer was so named because his butt was a broad as a beam. It's said that on every hog hunt there is a "bubba," a man who will never be a Mensa candidate, and on this hunt Beamer was that man. Luke had played quarterback for the high school football team, and just riding with a football hero increased Beamer's self-esteem. Penn went with them as well. The priest's intuition told him Lucius was the gentler of the two leaders, and since he was one of the six who hadn't hunted hogs, he wanted to subject himself to as little ridicule as possible. Bringing up the rear was Colby Young, an older man and friend of Hayden's. Colby was an experienced hog hunter.

The sun rose fast, gleaming yellow above gray and black bare tree limbs. Its warmth released the rich smells of the forest. The men rode quietly. Blue Jays and cardinals, mocking birds and wrens darted from tree to tree, from limb to limb above them, screaming and singing. Hawks floated lazily above the treetops, following the riders, hoping for leftovers from the hunt. Deer families were visible searching for grass under the fallen leaves, ignoring the riders; they didn't know why the men were in the forest, but they knew it wasn't their season. The horses almost strolled through the woods. Frances picked her way expertly. Luke rode her easily, holding the reins loosely; she needed no direction from him. He had on all of his RealTree winter camouflage, and was beginning to sweat. He wondered how Lucius and Colby managed to look so cool in their long leather coats. Suddenly, the dogs barked in the distance. They howled and bayed. They cried with joy. They spied a hog.

Now there was no need for the antenna, the dogs were making such a racket. "They got a hawg!" Lucius hollered. "Let's go!"

He raced off into the deeper brush and the rest of the riders followed him. Luke was surprised when Frances took off like a rocket; it seemed to take seconds for his body to catch up with her. She darted and wove her way around trees and through brush as if she were cutting cattle. Now Luke knew why quarter horses were the horse of choice for hog hunting. He was amazed; he sat on her easily, almost effortlessly.

As fast as Luke was going, Penn and Chester careened around him. Luke got a quick look at Penn's face as they passed; the expression was one of terror. Chester was running away, completely out of control. Penn's right foot had slipped out of the stirrup and he was looking down, struggling to get it back in. Before Luke could holler for help from Lucius, who was still ahead of them, Chester spied a low tree limb and ran straight for it. Luke screamed, "Penn, watch out!" but it was too late, and poor Penn probably couldn't have done anything if he'd seen it coming. Chester picked up even more speed and ran Penn straight into it. Lucius turned when he heard the loud "**thunk**" as Penn was knocked out of the saddle and over Chester's rear end. "Good Lord!" Lucius exclaimed, trying to reach out and grab Chester as he raced by. It was no use. The horse was gone.

The heavy man fell on his fat and rolled on the soft, leaf-covered Delta soil. Luke was the first to get to him; he almost jumped off Frances. "Lie still," he said. "Let's see if anything's broken."

"Goddamn it! Get away from me," Penn almost screamed. "I'm fine!" He pushed Luke away and sat up, brushing leaves and twigs from his camouflage suit.

Lucius rode up and looked down at Penn from atop his huge, white mare. "What the hell happened?"

"The goddamn horse ran away. Who brought that goddamn horse anyway?"

Lucius laughed. "That's Graber's horse. He wanted somebody to break it in for 'im."

Colby joined the group atop his mount, and laughed, "I guess you broke 'im in all right, Penn."

Beamer rode up laughing. Now that Luke knew Penn was all right, he couldn't help it; he laughed.

Penn stood up slowly. His leg hurt awfully, but he wasn't about to let these men know it. He looked down as he brushed more debris off, so he wouldn't have to see their faces. This was exactly what he feared more than anything, this was what he had nightmares about; a group of men laughing at him.

"Penn don't move!" Colby whispered, ice in his voice.

"He's right, don't move," Luke breathed. He, too, saw the huge rattler, just to the right of Penn's right foot. It must have been hiding under the leaves and Penn's fall uncovered it.

Penn immediately saw that the men were serious. He became a statue. Colby slowly, quietly pulled his rifle out of the holster, aimed and fired. The big snake jumped once, then was still. "You got him," Beamer beamed.

Penn looked down at the rattler. It was over five feet long, and fat as a Christmas goose. His knees turned to jelly. His second worse nightmare was being bitten by a poisonous snake. He managed to croak, "Thanks. That's a big mother."

"What'r we gonna' do with it?" Beamer asked.

"We're gonna' take it home and fry it up," Lucius answered. "Hand it up to me, Penn."

Penn reached down to get the headless snake, trying not to show the revulsion he felt. He grabbed it around the middle and slung it up to Lucius, who deftly caught it and draped it around his saddle horn. The dogs continued to bark in the distance. "How the hell am I gonna' hunt?" he asked no one and everyone.

"We've gotta' get Chester," Lucius answered. "He can't run around in the woods with a saddle on. He'll get hurt."

"Well, that would break my heart," Penn opined.

"Come on up with me," Colby said, reaching an arm down to Penn. "You can ride on Charlie's butt till we find your mount."

"I'm never getting on that damned horse again, even if we do find it." Penn caught hold of Colby's arm and the back of the saddle, pulling and struggling onto Charlie's backside. His leg felt better; it didn't seem broken after all.

Lucius was still laughing. "When we find Chester, I'll let you ride Sara. If you give her her head she won't run you into any trees. I can keep Chester under control." The group rode off in the direction of the baying dogs, which luckily was the direction Chester took. "Luke, use the walkie-talkie and tell Hayden and Jake to keep an eye out for Chester, and call us if they see him." Lucius turned on his own device and radioed Graber. "Penn let Chester run him into a tree," he laughed into the instrument. "If ya'll see him, let us know." The men heard Graber's laughter through the radio.

They couldn't ride as fast now with both Penn and Colby on Charlie, but it didn't matter. The dogs were barking like crazy, but the sound wasn't moving; they had a hog cornered. The sound of the dogs grew louder as the riders approached. The trees thinned out; the hog was in thick brush and sticker vines. Hogs are smart like B'er Rabbit. When chased, if they can, they run into the briar patch.

The mass of brush was too thick for the horses. Someone was going to have to crawl in and shoot the animal. Lucius looked around at his colleagues with a sly grin. "Who's gonna crawl in and pop 'im?" Usually either the youngest or the "bubba" in the group volunteered.

Luke looked at Colby, who was looking up at the soaring hawks, pretending not to be interested in the proceedings. Beamer looked at Luke, expecting the football hero to grab the honor.

Everyone was surprised when Penn spoke up. "I'll go." He saw this as his chance to recoup some respect. And, having never hunted boar before, he had no idea what he was in for. He threw his leg over Charlie's tail and slid down to the ground. It felt good to stand on solid earth again.

Lucius was both surprised and doubtful. "Are you sure you wanna' to do this, Rev.?" he asked with all good intentions. He didn't want to see the preacher killed, and certainly didn't want to carry any degree of responsibility for it if he were.

"That's what we're here for, isn't it?" Penn was slightly insulted by Lucius' tone, and somewhat surprised himself that he was the only one who seemed to want to bring the hunt to its natural climax. "So, what do I do?"

"Well," Lucius drawled, "you gotta' to crawl in on your hands 'n' knees. The hog's in the thickest part o' the brush, with the dogs all around 'im. He's mad, so you need to get off your best shot quick. If you wing 'im, he might charge."

"It looks like there's a good place over here to crawl in," Luke advised. Frances danced around, snorting, tired of standing in one place.

"Thanks," Penn muttered. Now that he had a clearer understanding of the requirements, he was less committed to carrying them out. He walked slowly over to the gap in the brush Luke pointed to. The hog or one of the larger dogs had probably gone in there. He heard their loud barking deep in the brush. The hog was silent. Penn pulled his pistol out of its holder and slipped it back in. He didn't let the men see he was praying.

He got down on hands and knees in front of the opening in the brush. Although the sun was bright overhead, inside the brush everything was dark. He saw little ahead of him except for more bare, tangled twigs and briar vines. Penn suddenly remembered an old joke; a young seminary student thinks God is calling him to preach in the Delta, but he isn't sure. His professor tells him to ask God for direction, saying if God means for him to go to the Delta, God will go with him. The seminarian prays, asking God if he should go to the Delta, and if He'll go with him. God answers, *"Yes, son, and I'll go with you as far as Yazoo city."* Penn asked himself, "What in heaven's name am I doing in this briar patch?" But, pride goeth before a fall, and Penn had his share of it. He crawled on into the brush.

The stickers grabbed off his hat and scratched his head, cheeks and hands. He felt blood and fire rise in the welts. It seemed hot as hell in the brush. Suddenly, the memory of the rattlesnake popped into his mind's eye. He jerked his head around to each side, and checked behind him. He felt somehow there should be a snake, but none was apparent. He sweated. He crawled forward, toward the sound of the barking. Now one dog's voice stood out. He must be getting close. Yes, there it was! It was Rambo. And just ahead of him was the hog. Penn had never seen a wild boar. He had a picture of a hog in his mind, but the animal he pictured was about two feet tall and weighed about a hundred pounds. The black boar he saw in the brush must have been three feet tall and weighed about 500 pounds. Its tusks rose out of its jaw over six inches. "Holy mother of God," Penn thought.

The hog was looking at the dog. Penn pulled the pistol out of the holster. "A good shot," he thought, smiling, aiming for the hog's head. "I'm in just the right place for a perfect shot. There'll be plenty of pork roast for supper tonight!" He pulled the trigger just as the hog decided to charge Rambo. The bullet hit the huge animal's shoulder and bounced off. No one had told Penn hogs have armor plate one and a half inches thick on the shoulders to protect them from the briars. Penn panicked when he saw the bullet ricochet off, and crazily thought the hog was bulletproof all over. And now, it was coming in his direction.

Rambo ran in front of the charging hog, trying to do his duty and protect the stupid human. The hog hit him a glancing blow with a tusk, slicing Rambo's skin along his rib cage. The hog came on. Penn dropped his gun and scurried backwards as fast as he could. Sticker vines ripped into his skin but he didn't notice. All he could see was 500 ponds of black hog and gleaming white tusks charging directly in front of his face. He moved more quickly than ever before, and broke through the brush just as the hog caught up to him. Penn rolled to the side as the enraged animal ran out into the clearing. The hunters on their horses were so surprised they couldn't get their guns out fast enough to shoot the terrified boar before it disappeared into the woods.

The dogs came out, sniffing around, wondering where the hog was they worked so hard to corner. They, too, were looking forward to pork for supper, at least the fat and bones. Seeing no carcass, they looked up at Lucius questioningly.

Lucius saw Rambo's bleeding side. "Goddamn some'bitch, what'id that hawg do to you, ole' boy?" He jumped down to minister to his lead hog dog, mildly irritated at Penn not only for losing their hog but for allowing his dog to get hurt. "Why didn't you shoot'em?" he sensibly asked.

Penn had pulled himself into a sitting position, trying to wipe the blood, sweat and tears from his face before the others got a good look at him. Until now, everyone had been occupied with the retreating hog and the dogs. "Goddamn it, I did! The bullet bounced right off him. Why didn't you tell me you couldn't kill a hog with a pistol? I thought you could kill a hog with a pistol. Ever body said you could." Penn stopped himself, feeling that if he continued he might begin to blubber. He ran his sleeve under his nose, and cringed when he saw his bloody hands. Not wanting to look at his tormentors, he looked up into the bright February sun and saw the circling hawks. Suddenly, he was overcome with peace.

"You're bleedin'." Luke said.

Penn laughed. "If you don't bleed, you didn't have fun," he said, then wondered where in the world the thought came from. He had never felt so peaceful before. He realized it didn't matter to him what the men thought. He had come through the valley of the shadow of death and God protected him. Although he preached that truth, he hadn't really expected God would, at least, not him, personally. "What do we do now?" he smiled up at Lucius.

The old hunter couldn't help being taken aback by Penn's attitude. "Well, we can't do much with you with no horse. We'd better radio Hayden n' Jake n' tell'em to come get ya'."

Luke called his dad on the walkie-talkie. Hayden and Jake weren't too far away, and found their way to the clearing. Lucius wanted to know if they had seen any sign of Chester, but they hadn't. Hayden said they'd call a friend with an airplane and get him to look for the errant horse the next day if they didn't find him. Lucius said he guessed the horse would learn a good lesson if he had to stay in the woods all night alone.

Luke decided he'd had enough hunting for one day. "I think I'll just ride along behind ya'll," he said. "We need to dig a pit in case Graber'n his bunch got a hog."

"You're right," Lucius said. "I need to clean up this slice on Rambo's side. Let's go in."

Over the sound of the engine, the riders heard laughter from the men in the jeep. Penn was telling the story start to finish, and Hayden and Jake laughed until their stomachs hurt. Back at the house, the riders dismounted and fed and watered their horses. Hayden, Jake, Luke and Penn dug a pit in the soft black Mississippi soil on the bluff overlooking the river. Before long, they heard the sound of horses' hooves and dogs barking. Graber and his crew came in, dragging a hog almost as big as the one that got away.

"Did you get a hawg?" Beamer asked, although the answer was obvious, his eyes big as saucers.

"Did we hunt?" Graber said smugly, sliding down his horse and pulling out his knife.

Luke decided he'd rather help with the horses than the butchering, and by time the animals were rubbed down, watered and fed, and the tack was put up, the pork was roasting in the pit.

Hayden and Jake went inside and brought out chairs. Colby came out behind them, carrying a sack full of paper plates, drink cups and plastic knives and forks. Luke and Beamer brought out huge bowls of potato salad and rolls their wives and mothers made for them. While the pork was cooking, Lucius had battered and fried up the rattlesnake, saying it tastes just like chicken. Coolers filled with beer and a few Cokes sat around the pit; bottles of bourbon rested beside them. Everyone was starving, and they sat down to eat and drink into the night.

Suddenly it occurred to Beamer to ask, "Lucius, did you cut the poison part out of that snake before you cooked it?"

"Goddamn, I forgot to," Lucius said, looking scared.

"Oh, no!" Beamer hollered, getting up and grabbing his stomach. "We're all gonna die! Call 911!"

"Oh, sit down," Hayden said. Can't you tell Lucius is just kidding?"

"Oh," Beamer said, sitting down as he was told, but still scared, not sure now exactly who was telling the truth.

It got dark and chilly early. One by one the stars came out over the great river. The men made Penn tell his story again and again. He didn't drink as much as usual, saying he wanted to feel his pain and relish his wounds. In the light from the pit's glowing embers, the men told lies and talked about Robert E. Lee and the Civil War. Luke looked out at the dark water; at night, the Mississippi was so wide you couldn't see to the other side. He imagined a black Yankee iron clad slipping silently down the river towards Vicksburg. And the dogs slept, snoring, heads over the men's legs, bellies full of pork fat.

**Louise Jaffe**
**Brooklyn, New York**

## Hostess

Like a character fit for a Kafka novel
or a Beckett play
I ask whether he likes the pie I've bought
for his between-brunch-and-dinner-with-others visit
his day-off thin time-slice
of his incredibly separate life.

He seems too busy eating the pie
to realize how weird my question tastes,
how it squats in my throat
like a tablespoon of something
not quite digested.
I wish he could share
his immunity.


As an invisible
and silent expectation,
he ate whatever I did
without being asked for
or equipped to give
his opinion.

Later
after we'd become two
I stuffed him
according to the doctor's suggestions
as if they had descended
from Mount Sinai
until
with the enigma of years' fast forwarding
he usurped the words
to let me know
beyond most cajoling
what he liked
and hated
to eat.

But now
in the same kitchen
where I fed him

such a heap of years ago
I hunger from my amnesia
about the menus
especially the desserts
and from the oceans
between us
so clearly mapped
beneath my wrinkling skin.


                              * * *


## Request in Absentia

Let me remember the lilacs, Momma
instead of the gut-churning cabals
of *your* near-daily Jeremiads
about our money-lacks
real or lent life
by *your* obsession-stretched
imaginings.

Let me remember these birthday markings
my mid-May re-welcomings
to a world that *you* wordlessly limned
all the less-magic days
as too sadness-stained
too bill-sick
to need
or have  even one drop of time
for my breaths.

Let me remember
this short-lived specialness
this sweetness wafting through
whatever low-rent apartment
that birthday found us in.

Let me remember the perfumed spell
of Princess-for-a-Daydom,
last year's vase
cradling what I yearn to taste
as that year's love.

Let me remember the lilacs, Momma

in full bloom.
Let me forget
their too-quick withering.
So many other deaths
and silenced dreams,
so many gray days later,
is this too much
to ask?

*Linda Hudson Hoaglund*
*North Tazewell, VA*

# The Trouble With Ellen

There was a small family graveyard located on the hillside above the barn that wasn't used anymore, at least, not to inter members of the Johnson family that were currently living on the property. The ancestors weren't those of the Johnson's so they saw no need to maintain the graveyard.

Ellen, who was eight years old and known for snooping around when she shouldn't, didn't like the idea of not mowing the grass and weeding around the headstones. She thought it was something that should be done but she didn't want to be the one to do it. She didn't like graveyards not one little bit.

"Mom, why doesn't someone take care of those graves like they do in big cemeteries?"

"I don't know. Maybe all of the members of that branch of the Hudson family are dead and there is no one left living to do the mowing and weeding."

"I don't think so. Nancy told me the son of Delbert and Molly Hudson lives in town. He should be looking after those graves, shouldn't he?"

"You would think that he would do that but maybe his health won't allow him to."

"Couldn't he pay somebody to do it?"

"Maybe he can't afford to."

"Nancy says he loaded, got lots of money."

"Nancy is eight years old and goes to your school. How does she know so much about this man?"

"Her mommy used to date him, that's how."

"What's his name?"

"Kenny Hudson and he's never been married and Nancy says he is really strange."

"Strange? How?"

"I don't really know, but if Nancy says he's strange, I believe her."

"If you're so worried about that graveyard, why don't you take care of the graves?"

"Me? I'm scared of graveyards."

"Why? The people buried in them are already dead. They can't hurt you?" said Ellen's mother as she laughed.

"I know, I know," said Ellen as she looked down at her feet in embarrassment.

"You've been watching too many scary movies on television, Young Lady. I'm not going to let you watch those things any more."

"No, Mom, you can't do that. I love to watch those movies."

"Then you shouldn't mind taking care of those graves, should you?"

"I guess not," said Ellen as she watched her foot that she was poking out in front of her.

"We'll both go up there tomorrow. I'll take the lawnmower and mow the grass. You can pull the weeds around each headstone. There's only four in there. It shouldn't take us more than half a day to get it back into order and looking like it should look."

Ellen went to bed with the graveyard weighing heavily on her mind. She shouldn't have mentioned it to her mother because she was going to have to do what she really didn't want to do. Graveyards gave her the willies. Just walking passed one made chills run up and down her spine.

Her dreams were filled with the dead rising up from the earth. They held their arms outstretched in front of them like zombies and walked stiff legged like Frankenstein. Their eyes were holes that pulled you into their dark depths to see the world of maggots and worms crawling around inside the ugly outside shell. One of them reached for her. Ellen started running as fast as her short legs would carry her.

"No, get away!" Ellen screamed as she woke herself up from the night-mare.

"Ellen, are you all right?" asked her concerned mother.

"I'm fine. Just a bad dream, mom. Go on back to bed."

Ellen turned on her lamp that was sitting on her nightstand and looked at her twisted blanket.

"That's what running in bed will do to you," she mumbled as she tried to rearrange her bed linens so she could go back to sleep without any more dreams, she hoped.

Bright and early the next morning, which had to be a Saturday, the one day that Ellen wanted to sleep late, she was roused from her bed to begin the graveyard cleanup.

"Why so early, Mom?"

"I've got a lot to do today. It's Halloween and I want to make sure things are tied down or locked up before the trick or treating begins. The kids around here are liable to do anything they think is funny. Last year old Mr. Hanson's out-house was knocked over. Thank goodness he wasn't using it at the time. A couple of years before that Mr. Foster's cow was painted green. Poor thing died, the cow I mean."

"Do you think they'll do anything like that to our stuff?"

"I certainly hope not. I don't want to give them a chance to do it so that's why I'll put everything behind lock and key that I can."

"Those kids are mean."

"No, they really aren't mean. They just didn't think about what would happen if they painted the cow green."

"Do we have to clean up the graveyard today?"

"Yes, we do. I want you to see that no harm will come to you if you do something good for people even when they're dead."

Ellen helped her mother gather the tools they needed and put them in a box for Ellen to carry. Her mother pushed the lawnmower up the hillside which seemed to be miles away before they came to gate that opened up into the cemetery.

"Ellen, you cut some of the tall, thick weeds with this hedge trimmer. Just be careful. I'll see about getting the mower started. Watch for snakes or anything that might be crawling on the ground. You never know what kind of creature you might run into in a place like this."

Ellen's eyes widened with fright.

"I'm talking about living creatures not dead ones, Ellen."

"I know," Ellen said sullenly as she started scissoring the hedge trimmers at some tall weeds.

Ellen was tense and nervous as she whacked away at the tall weeds with the hedge trimmers. As her arms grew tired of the constant scissoring motion, she stopped whacking and started pulling the weeds from the headstones.

She had actually located all four of the stones and noticed that each grave marker had words painted on the stone, not etched as she had seen on the grave markers in other cemeteries that she had been compelled to visit because of some family member or friend of her parents dying. It was usually someone she didn't even know so she paid more attention to her surroundings than she did to the actual funeral ceremony.

The stones didn't look like the same kind of stones that were in those other cemeteries. They weren't glazed and polished like she had always seen them. They were shaped like headstones but they looked home made, not the kind that most people purchased from catalogs from the grave marker store.

Her mother cut away at the grass with the lawnmower, which was a hard job. She had to cut narrow strips of the tall grass so the mower wouldn't stall out from trying to bite off more than it could chew up and spit out.

Finally the lawnmower had done all it could do and the rest of the work had to be performed by hand.

Ellen and her mother pulled and yanked at weeds around each of the four headstones and when they had finally reached a point where they were happy with the work they had done, they started reading the words that were painted on them for the world to see.

The first headstone they read said:

DELBERT HUDSON
An Ugly Old Goat
Died: June 3, 1978

The walked to the second headstone and read:

MOLLY HUDSON
A Really Mean Bitch
Died: April 22, 1970

Ellen and her mother returned to the house and tried to puzzle out what they had discovered in the graveyard.

"Mom, are those the graves of Kenny Hudson's mom and dad?"

"I don't know, Ellen."

"Why would he write on the headstones that his dad was an ugly old goat and that his mom was a really mean bitch?" she asked with a puzzled tone. "Why would anyone put that on a grave marker? That sure would be mean, don't you think?"

"We probably need to talk to Mr. Kenny Hudson to find out why he did that. I will look his number up in the telephone book when we get back to the house. I would like to give Mr. Kenny Hudson a piece of my mind for making markers like that for his parents," said Ellen's mom as she tried to control her temper.

"Go get me the phone book, Ellen. I'm calling Mr. Kenny Hudson right now," she said angrily as she walked into the house.

"Can I listen?"

"Sure, you need to know the answer as much as I do."

Ellen's mother dialed the only Kenneth Hudson listed in the book.

"Mr. Hudson? Mr. Kenneth Hudson?"

"Yes?"

"I'm Martha Johnson. I'm living in the house that was once owned by your mother and father. We are renting it through Regency Rentals. I've got you on the speaker phone so my daughter can hear what we say to each other."

"If you're having any problem with the house, you need to call Regency Rentals," he said hurriedly. "I let them handle all of that. Good by...."

"Mr. Hudson, I'm not calling about the house," said Ellen's mother before Kenny Hudson hung up the phone.

"What is it then?" he said apprehensively.

"It's about the cemetery."

"What about it?"

"Why do you not take care of the graves of your mother and father?"

"I don't have to. I pay people to do that."

"They are not doing a very good job of it. As a matter of fact, they haven't even mowed the grass around the grave markers. Did you make the markers yourself?"

"What are you talking about? I saw the graves of my parents last week and they looked fine. The grass was mowed and the area had been weeded."

"When did you visit the graves?"

"Last week. I saw them last week."

"I didn't see you. What time do you stop by the house?"

"I went to the cemetery last week. I didn't go to the house. I haven't been to the house for a very long time."

"Wait a minute, wait a minute," said Ellen's mom, "I don't think we are talking about the same thing. I'm talking about the cemetery on the hill by the house that your parents owned. That little cemetery has four graves in it with four headstones. My daughter and I just mowed the grass and uncovered the stones."

"Oh, that's what you're talking about."

"Yes, Mr. Hudson. Why would you call your father, Delbert Hudson, an old goat, and your mother, Molly Hudson, a mean bitch?"

"Because that's what they were. The old goat was an old goat, not my dad. The mean bitch was a dog. I named them Delbert and Molly because I loved them like I loved my mom and dad."

"You mean it's a pet cemetery?"

"Yes, Mrs. Johnson. All four the graves were for family pets."

"Thank you, Mr. Hudson, you'll be happy to know that the pet cemetery is ship shape and looking good. Goodbye."

Martha Johnson disconnected the call.

"Ellen, I guess we were both wrong, weren't we?"

"Maybe that explains the howling dog I hear at night and the goat I see walking across the hill every once in a while."

"What are you talking about?"

"They are the remaining ghosts of the Hudson family."

"I've never heard a howling dog or seen a wandering goat."

"I have."

Ellen went to her room to take a nap. It had been an exhausting morning. Besides, she wanted to rest up to go trick or treating with her friends.

\* \* \*

**Sheryl L. Nelms**
**Azle TX**

## On Medicine Bow Mountain

Rocky Mountain iris
blooms sprinkle blue

through meadow grass

tiddlehead ferns
unfurl green spirals
along the creek

aspen leaves
tremor

in the silken breeze

mountain jay
squawks
echo

across Medicine Bow Canyon

as rainbow trout
jump

for May flies

the quick
slap

of beaver tail

ripples warning
rings over
the pond

\* \* \*


## Downed Hawk

wings drooping

he huddles
beside the highway

like a defeated
Apache

chief

under a
reservation
blanket


*E. Leynes Bautista*

## Fairy tales

She satisfied her hunger
For excitement with playfulness s
wirling around the children's carousel
Like a sliver of blue sky.

That was before her muscle wasting pains
Sapped her strength and stopped
The rasping skid of her walker.
That was before the blooming of her mind
Was ravaged by cognitive decline.
Her baby steps of long ago

Came full circle when she cried.

I rocked her
While she jerked with restlessness
And calmed her with lullabyes.
I kept vigil
In a bedroom full of plumage
Where she once eased
Our children to sleep.
Can the twinkling stars of fairy tales
Momentarily open her eyes
Here in a playroom full of dolls, '
What we lost in beauty'
Whispered one, 'we find in love.'

\* \* \*

## Kelley Jean White
## Philadelphia,

## Solstice

The last time I can remember that my husband showed love for me
it was like this: he was kept late at the hospital; when he came home
I was walking the dog at midnight on the November street;
he hurried to take the leash from me, pushed an arm around my shoulder—
"there's a madman loose in the city preying on women alone."

His case was this: two women had been killed and a third damaged,
quite probably beyond hope. The Assailant's modus was to approach
a woman working alone in a small shop, smash her head with a brick,
and empty the cash register. The first was at a dry cleaners, the second
a mom & pop store, the third was a young woman working in her family's flower
shop.

The florist was alive. They had her in surgery for hours, picking skull fragments
from her brain. My husband, as plastic surgeon on call, was asked to tuck
what remained of her left ear beneath a flap of skin: later, it could be reconstructed,
later, if she survived. It felt trivial, while the neurosurgeons labored and orthopedics
pinned bone and general surgeons stabilized bowel and spleen, but he did as
asked.

He followed her case closely though her management was not in his hands.
Remarkably, she showed small signs of improvement, a hint of recognition for
her husband, her small son. Quite uncharacteristicly, he went with me to Quaker
meeting.
A young man stood and sang Amazing Grace and spoke of a close friend's suicide

at the solstice a year before. Everyone spoke of fading, dying, loss of light.

He sat stirring beside me. I could see the tremble, the push that they say comes
from God to lead one to speak. He struggled. I thought he would stand. I watched
his face,
heard his breath quicken. He wanted to speak of miracles and hope. Of the small
things we do, seemingly
empty, that may mean more than we can dream. The leading
never cleared. The hour closed. They asked for those new to meeting to stand.

And a young woman rose in the front row, thin, knit cap pulled over shaven head
and hidden ear,
that woman rose and spoke to all of us her name.



\* \* \*

**Michael Fitzgerald**
**Winchester, VA**

## A Stand of Pines

The evergreens on the approach
to the old New Hampshire town
rise with stretch. and stillness
like a row of deacons.

This stand of pines,
a New England skyline,
traces and trims
the cumulus ,clouds above.

The conifers line the curve
and contour of road.
These venerable elders in green
enhance the very idea of stature.

Each tree points to the real,
enacted and ideal thing
we call the sky and holds a promise
made of generations in its quiet.

Printed in the United States
27644LVS00005B/28-84

9 780890 023778